A 21ST CENTURY
CYBER-PHYSICAL SYSTEMS
EDUCATION

Committee on 21st Century Cyber-Physical Systems Education

Computer Science and Telecommunications Board

Division on Engineering and Physical Sciences

A Report of

The National Academies of
SCIENCES · ENGINEERING · MEDICINE

THE NATIONAL ACADEMIES PRESS
Washington, DC
www.nap.edu

THE NATIONAL ACADEMIES PRESS   500 Fifth Street, NW   Washington, DC 20001

This activity was supported by Award No. CNS-1341078 from the National Science Foundation. Any opinions, findings, conclusions, or recommendations expressed in this publication do not necessarily reflect the views of any organization or agency that provided support for the project.

International Standard Book Number-13:   978-0-309-45163-5
International Standard Book Number-10:   0-309-45163-9
Digital Object Identifier: 10.17226/23686

Additional copies of this report are available for sale from the National Academies Press, 500 Fifth Street, NW, Keck 360, Washington, DC 20001; (800) 624-6242 or (202) 334-3313; http://www.nap.edu.

Copyright 2016 by the National Academy of Sciences. All rights reserved.

Printed in the United States of America

Suggested citation: National Academies of Sciences, Engineering, and Medicine. 2016. *A 21st Century Cyber-Physical Systems Education.* Washington, DC: The National Academies Press. doi:10.17226/23686.

The National Academies of
SCIENCES · ENGINEERING · MEDICINE

The **National Academy of Sciences** was established in 1863 by an Act of Congress, signed by President Lincoln, as a private, nongovernmental institution to advise the nation on issues related to science and technology. Members are elected by their peers for outstanding contributions to research. Dr. Marcia McNutt is president.

The **National Academy of Engineering** was established in 1964 under the charter of the National Academy of Sciences to bring the practices of engineering to advising the nation. Members are elected by their peers for extraordinary contributions to engineering. Dr. C. D. Mote, Jr., is president.

The **National Academy of Medicine** (formerly the Institute of Medicine) was established in 1970 under the charter of the National Academy of Sciences to advise the nation on medical and health issues. Members are elected by their peers for distinguished contributions to medicine and health. Dr. Victor J. Dzau is president.

The three Academies work together as the **National Academies of Sciences, Engineering, and Medicine** to provide independent, objective analysis and advice to the nation and conduct other activities to solve complex problems and inform public policy decisions. The National Academies also encourage education and research, recognize outstanding contributions to knowledge, and increase public understanding in matters of science, engineering, and medicine.

Learn more about the National Academies of Sciences, Engineering, and Medicine at **www.national-academies.org**.

The National Academies of
SCIENCES · ENGINEERING · MEDICINE

Reports document the evidence-based consensus of an authoring committee of experts. Reports typically include findings, conclusions, and recommendations based on information gathered by the committee and committee deliberations. Reports are peer reviewed and are approved by the National Academies of Sciences, Engineering, and Medicine.

Proceedings chronicle the presentations and discussions at a workshop, symposium, or other convening event. The statements and opinions contained in proceedings are those of the participants and have not been endorsed by other participants, the planning committee, or the National Academies of Sciences, Engineering, and Medicine.

For information about other products and activities of the National Academies, please visit nationalacademies.org/whatwedo.

COMMITTEE ON 21ST CENTURY CYBER-PHYSICAL SYSTEMS EDUCATION

JOHN A. (JACK) STANKOVIC, University of Virginia, *Co-Chair*
JAMES (JIM) STURGES, Lockheed Martin Corporation (retired), *Co-Chair*
ALEXANDRE BAYEN, University of California, Berkeley
CHARLES R. FARRAR, Los Alamos National Laboratory
MARYE ANNE FOX, NAS,[1] University of California, San Diego
SANTIAGO GRIJALVA, Georgia Institute of Technology
HIMANSHU KHURANA, Honeywell International, Inc.
P.R. KUMAR, NAE,[2] Texas A&M University, College Station
INSUP LEE, University of Pennsylvania
WILLIAM MILAM, Ford Motor Company
SANJOY K. MITTER, NAE, Massachusetts Institute of Technology
JOSÉ M.F. MOURA, NAE, Carnegie Mellon University
GEORGE J. PAPPAS, University of Pennsylvania
PAULO TABUADA, University of California, Los Angeles
MANUELA M. VELOSO, Carnegie Mellon University

Staff

JON EISENBERG, Director, Computer Science and Telecommunications Board
VIRGINIA BACON TALATI, Program Officer
SHENAE BRADLEY, Administrative Assistant
CHRISTOPHER JONES, Associate Program Officer

---

[1] NAS, National Academy of Sciences.
[2] NAE, National Academy of Engineering.

COMPUTER SCIENCE AND TELECOMMUNICATIONS BOARD

FARNAM JAHANIAN, Carnegie Mellon University, *Chair*
LUIZ ANDRE BARROSO, Google, Inc.
STEVEN M. BELLOVIN, NAE, Columbia University
ROBERT F. BRAMMER, Brammer Technology, LLC
EDWARD FRANK, Cloud Parity, Inc.
LAURA HAAS, NAE, IBM Corporation
MARK HOROWITZ, NAE, Stanford University
ERIC HORVITZ, NAE, Microsoft Research
VIJAY KUMAR, NAE, University of Pennsylvania
BETH MYNATT, Georgia Institute of Technology
CRAIG PARTRIDGE, Raytheon BBN Technologies
DANIELA RUS, NAE, Massachusetts Institute of Technology
FRED B. SCHNEIDER, NAE, Cornell University
MARGO SELTZER, Harvard University
JOHN STANKOVIC, University of Virginia
MOSCHE VARDI, NAS/NAE, Rice University
KATHERINE YELICK, University of California, Berkeley

Staff

JON EISENBERG, Director
LYNETTE I. MILLETT, Associate Director

VIRGINIA BACON TALATI, Program Officer
SHENAE BRADLEY, Administrative Assistant
JANEL DEAR, Senior Program Assistant
EMILY GRUMBLING, Program Officer
RENEE HAWKINS, Financial and Administrative Manager
CHRISTOPHER JONES, Associate Program Officer
KATIRIA ORTIZ, Research Associate

For more information on CSTB, see its website at http://www.cstb.org, write to CSTB, National Academies of Sciences, Engineering, and Medicine, 500 Fifth Street, NW, Washington, DC 20001, call (202) 334-2605, or e-mail the CSTB at cstb@nas.edu.

Preface

Cyber-physical systems (CPS) are "engineered systems that are built from, and depend upon, the seamless integration of computational algorithms and physical components."[1] CPS are increasingly relied on to provide the functionality and value of products, systems, and infrastructure in sectors such as transportation (aviation, automotive, rail, and marine), health care, manufacturing, and energy networks. Advances in CPS could yield systems that can communicate and respond faster than humans (e.g., autonomous collision avoidance for automobiles) or more precisely (e.g., robotic surgery); enable better control and coordination of large-scale systems, such as the electrical grid or traffic controls; improve the efficiency of systems (e.g., smart buildings); and enable advances in many areas of science (e.g. autonomous telescopes that capture astronomical transients). Cyber-physical systems have the potential to provide much richer functionality—including efficiency, flexibility, autonomy, and reliability—than systems that are loosely coupled, discrete, or manually operated, but CPS also can create vulnerability related to security and reliability.

Building on its research program in CPS, the National Science Foundation (NSF) has begun to explore requirements for education and training for CPS. As part of that exploration, NSF asked the National Acad-

---

[1] Definition from National Science Foundation, 2016, "Cyber-Physical Systems," program solicitation 16-549, NSF document number nsf16549, March 4. https://www.nsf.gov/publications/pub_summ.jsp?ods_key=nsf16549.

> **BOX P.1**
> **Statement of Task**
>
> An ad hoc committee will conduct a study on the current and future needs in education for cyber-physical systems (CPS). Two workshops would be convened early on to gather input and foster dialogue, and a brief interim report would be prepared to highlight emerging themes and summarize related discussions from the workshops. The committee's final report would articulate a vision for a 21st century CPS-capable U.S. workforce. It would explore the corresponding educational requirements, examine efforts already under way, and propose strategies and programs to develop faculty and teachers, materials, and curricula. It would consider core, cross-domain, and domain-specific knowledge. It would consider the multiple disciplines that are relevant to CPS and how to foster multidisciplinary study and work. In conducting the study, the committee would focus on undergraduate education and also consider implications for graduate education, workforce training and certification, community colleges, the K-12 pipeline, and informal education. It would emphasize the skills needed for the CPS scientific, engineering, and technical workforce but would also consider broader needs for CPS survey courses.

emies of Sciences, Engineering, and Medicine to study the topic, organize workshops, and prepare interim and final reports examining the need for and content of a CPS education (Box P-1). The results of this study are intended to inform those who might support efforts to develop curricula and materials (including but not limited to NSF); faculty and university administrators; industries with needs for CPS workers; and current and potential students about intellectual foundations, workforce requirements, employment opportunities, and curricular needs.

The report examines the intellectual content of the emerging field of CPS and its implications for engineering and computer science education. Other National Academies reports have examined broader related topics such as the future of engineering education more generally[2] and how to overcome barriers to completing 2- and 4-year science, technology, engineering, and mathematics degrees.[3]

To gather perspectives on these topics, the Committee on 21st Century Cyber-Physical Systems Education (committee biographical informa-

---

[2] National Academy of Engineering, 2005, *Educating the Engineer of 2020: Adapting Engineering Education to the New Century*, The National Academies Press, Washington, D.C.

[3] National Academies of Sciences, Engineering, and Medicine, *Barriers and Opportunities for 2-Year and 4-Year STEM Degrees: Systemic Change to Support Diverse Student Pathways* (S. Malcom and M. Feder, eds.), The National Academies Press, Washington, D.C., 2016, doi: 10.17226/21739.

tion is provided in Appendix A) convened two workshops and received briefings from additional experts (all presenters and briefers are listed in Appendix B, and the workshop agendas are provided in Appendix C). The committee's interim report,[4] released in 2015, summarizes many of those presentations and discussions. This final report also draws on an additional set of briefings (listed in Appendix B) obtained since the interim report was issued. Informed by these inputs as well as a review of current CPS courses, course materials, and curricula and other information compiled for this study, the committee's findings and recommendations are based on the committee's collective judgment.

The key messages of the reports and the committee's findings and recommendations are presented in the Summary. Chapter 1 of this report explores the need for CPS education, and Chapter 2 highlights the essential knowledge and skills needed by a person developing CPS. Chapter 3 provides examples of how these foundations in CPS education might be integrated into various curricula, and Chapter 4 discusses how such curricula might be developed and institutionalized.

> Jack Stankovic and Jim Sturges, *Co-Chairs*
> Committee on 21st Century Cyber-Physical Systems Education

---

[4] National Academies of Sciences, Engineering, and Medicine, *Interim Report on 21st Century Cyber-Physical Systems Education*, The National Academies Press, Washington, D.C., 2015.

Acknowledgment of Reviewers

This report has been reviewed in draft form by individuals chosen for their diverse perspectives and technical expertise. The purpose of this independent review is to provide candid and critical comments that will assist the institution in making its published report as sound as possible and to ensure that the report meets institutional standards for objectivity, evidence, and responsiveness to the study charge. The review comments and draft manuscript remain confidential to protect the integrity of the deliberative process. We wish to thank the following individuals for their review of this report:

Ella M. Atkins, University of Michigan,
Robert F. Brammer, Brammer Technology, LLC,
Harry H. Cheng, University of California, Davis,
Elsa M. Garmire, NAE,[1] Dartmouth College,
Scott Hareland, Medtronics,
Mats P. Heimdahl, University of Minnesota, Minneapolis,
Ken Hoyme, Adventium Labs,
Edward A. Lee, University of California, Berkeley,
Jerome P. Lynch, University of Michigan,
Alberto Sangiovanni-Vincentelli, University of California, Berkeley,
Robert F. Sproull, NAE, University of Massachusetts, and
Yannis C. Yortsos, NAE, University of Southern California.

---

[1] NAE, National Academy of Engineering.

Although the reviewers listed above have provided many constructive comments and suggestions, they were not asked to endorse the conclusions or recommendations, nor did they see the final draft of the report before its release. The review of this report was overseen by Philip M. Neches, Teradata Corporation, and Samuel H. Fuller, Analog Devices, Inc., who were responsible for making certain that an independent examination of this report was carried out in accordance with institutional procedures and that all review comments were carefully considered. Responsibility for the final content of this report rests entirely with the authoring committee and the institution.

Contents

SUMMARY   1

1   THE TRANSFORMATIVE NATURE OF CPS AND WORKFORCE NEEDS   13
The Transformative Nature of CPS, 13
Building a CPS Workforce, 18
CPS: An Emerging Engineering Discipline, 22

2   CPS PRINCIPLES, FOUNDATIONS, SYSTEM CHARACTERISTICS, AND COMPLEMENTARY SKILLS   24
Principles: Integrating the Physical and Cyber, 25
Foundations of CPS, 27
System Characteristics, 30
Complementary Skills, 32

3   PATHS TO CPS KNOWLEDGE   34
Overview of Relevant Existing Paths and Programs to CPS Expertise, 36
K-12 Education Programs, 38
Vocational and Community Colleges, 39
Undergraduate Courses, Concentrations, and Programs, 40
Graduate Degree Programs, 59

4	DEVELOPING AND INSTITUTIONALIZING CPS CURRICULA	60

Drawing Students to CPS, 60
Recruiting, Retaining, and Developing the Needed Faculty, 62
Curriculum Development and Resources, 65
Fostering Development of the CPS Discipline and CPS
  Education, 67

APPENDIXES

A	Biographies of Committee Members and Staff	71
B	Briefers to the Study Committee	82
C	Workshop Agendas	84

Summary

Cyber-physical systems (CPS) are "engineered systems that are built from, and depend upon, the seamless integration of computational algorithms and physical components."[1] CPS can be small and closed, such as an artificial pancreas, or very large, complex, and interconnected, such as a regional energy grid. CPS engineering[2] focuses on managing interdependencies and impact of physical aspects on cyber aspects, and vice versa. With the development of low-cost sensing, powerful embedded system hardware, and widely deployed communication networks, the reliance on CPS for system functionality has dramatically increased. These technical developments in combination with the creation of a workforce skilled in engineering CPS will allow the deployment of increasingly capable, adaptable, and trustworthy systems.

CPS ENGINEERING AND THE CPS WORKFORCE

CPS are already widely deployed and used today. Examples include automobiles that sense impending crashes and perform various tasks to

---

[1] Definition from National Science Foundation, 2016, "Cyber-Physical Systems," Program Solicitation 16-549, NSF document number nsf16549, March 4, https://www.nsf.gov/publications/pub_summ.jsp?ods_key=nsf16549.

[2] The committee uses the terms "CPS engineering" and "CPS engineer" to mean a set of skills and knowledge needed to design and build a CPS and a person with those skills; the terms are not limited to a set of credentials or to someone who has a degree or certification in CPS.

protect passengers and medical devices that sense glucose levels or the heart's rhythm and intervene to restore normal body function. As these examples illustrate, CPS often support critical missions that have significant economic and societal importance and raise significant safety and cybersecurity concerns. However, today's practice of CPS system design and implementation is often ad hoc, not taking advantage of even the limited theory that exists today, and unable to support the level of complexity, scalability, security, safety, interoperability, and flexible design and operation that will be required to meet future needs.

Engineers responsible for developing CPS but lacking the appropriate education or training may not fully understand at an appropriate depth, on the one hand, the technical issues associated with the CPS software and hardware or, on the other hand, techniques for physical system modeling, energy and power, actuation, signal processing, and control. In addition, these engineers may be designing and implementing life-critical systems without appropriate formal training in CPS methods needed for verification and to assure safety, reliability, and security.

A workforce with the appropriate education, training, and skills will be better positioned to create and manage the next generation of CPS solutions. Building this workforce will require attention to educating the future workforce with all the required skills—integrated from the ground up—as well as providing the existing workforce with the needed supplementary education.

It proved difficult to obtain comprehensive data on industrial demand for CPS skills, and the committee was not in a position to commission systematic surveys to collect such information itself. Instead, the committee has relied on the perspectives of industry experts, including those who briefed the committee or who participated in the two workshops convened during its study. It was also apparent from these presentations that the CPS field will continue to evolve as new applications emerge and as more research is done.

> **FINDING 1.1:** CPS are emerging as an area of engineering with significant economic and societal implications. Major industrial sectors such as transportation, medicine, energy, defense, and information technology increasingly need a workforce capable of designing and engineering products and services that intimately combine cyber elements (computing hardware and software) and physical components and manage their interactions and impact on the physical environment. Although it is difficult to quantify the demand, a likely implication is that more CPS-capable engineers will be needed.

FINDING 1.2: The future CPS workforce is likely to include a combination of (1) engineers trained in foundational fields (such as electrical and computing engineering, mechanical engineering, systems engineering, and computer science); (2) engineers trained in specific applied engineering fields (such as aerospace and civil engineering); and (3) CPS engineers, who focus on the knowledge and skills spanning cyber technology and physical systems that operate in the physical world.

The mix of programs offered by universities will reflect the perspectives of individual institutions, their resources, and the demand universities see from students and their employers, and in turn affect the educational backgrounds of the CPS workforce. Over time, as the field itself changes and matures, education and employer demand will co-evolve.

FINDING 1.3: Given that most entry-level engineering and computer science positions are filled by undergraduates, it is important to incorporate CPS into the undergraduate engineering and computer science curricula.

RECOMMENDATION 1.1: The National Science Foundation, together with universities, should support the creation and evolution of undergraduate education courses, programs, and pathways so that engineering and computer science graduates have more opportunities to gain the knowledge and skills required to engineer cyber-physical systems. The efforts should be complemented by initiatives to augment the skills of the existing workforce through continuing education and master's degree programs.

CPS PRINCIPLES, FOUNDATIONS, SYSTEM CHARACTERISTICS, AND COMPLEMENTARY SKILLS

This section summarizes the knowledge and skills needed to engineer CPS. It is derived from an examination of existing courses, programs, and instructional materials as well as consideration of the topics highlighted in comments from industry experts. The emphasis is deliberately on core principles and foundations reflecting the challenge of packing the material needed to span both cyber and physical aspects into an already crowded engineering curricula.

The committee has identified the following four broad areas for CPS education programs to cover:

- *Principles* that define the integration of physical and cyber aspects in such areas as communication and networking, real-time operation, distributed and embedded systems, physical properties of hardware and the environment, and human interaction.
- *Foundations of CPS* in (1) basic computing concepts, (2) computing for the physical world, (3) discrete and continuous mathematics, (4) cross-cutting applications, (5) modeling, and (6) system development.
- *System characteristics* required of CPS, such as security and privacy; interoperability; reliability and dependability; power and energy management; safety; stability and performance of dynamic and stochastic systems; and human factors and usability.

Each area is briefly outlined in the sections below (and discussed in more detail in Chapter 2).

Principles

CPS bridges engineering and physical world applications and the computer engineering hardware and computer science cyber worlds. Basic principles of the physical world include physics, mathematical modeling, analysis, and algorithm and systems design and deal with their associated uncertainty and risk. Principles of the computer engineering and computer science (cyber) worlds deal with embedded computation and communications hardware systems, software programming, and networking, Because sensors are a key hardware bridge between the physical and cyber worlds, it is important to understand the properties of sensors and their real-world behavior, and techniques for processing the signals they produce. Control theory is an important tenet of CPS; relevant elements include stability, optimization, and how to control distributed, digital systems.

Foundations of CPS

Drawing on these principles, the committee identified the following six key overarching intellectual foundations for a CPS curriculum:

1. *Basic computing concepts* beyond those covered in a couple of introductory programming courses, such as embedded hardware, data structures, automata theory, and software engineering.
2. *Computing for the physical world*, which involves understanding physical world properties, real-time embedded systems, and computing resource constraints such as power and memory size.

3. *Discrete and continuous mathematics* beyond calculus, such as differential equations, probability and stochastic processes, and linear algebra.

4. *Cross-cutting application of sensing, actuation, control, communication, and computing* reflecting the central role of interactions between physical and cyber aspects and the reliance on control over communication networks, sensing, signal processing, and actuation with real-time constraints.

5. *Modeling of heterogeneous and dynamic systems integrating control, computing, and communication,* with emphasis on uncertainty and system heterogeneity, including such techniques as linear and nonlinear models, stochastic models, discrete-event and hybrid models, and associated design methodologies based on optimization, probability theory, and dynamic programming.

6. *CPS system development*, especially for safety-critical, high-confidence, and resilient systems, requires a life-cycle view from initial requirements to testing to certification and in-service use, including formal verification and validation procedures and adaptable designs that can accommodate system evolution.

FINDING 2.1: Core CPS knowledge involves not only an understanding of the basics of physical engineering and cyber design and implementation, but understanding how the physical and cyber aspects influence and affect each other.

RECOMMENDATION 2.1: Cyber-physical systems educational programs should provide a foundation that highlights the interaction of cyber and physical aspects of systems. Most current courses fail to emphasize the interaction, implying that new courses and instructional materials are needed.

System Characteristics

Many CPS are large, complex, and/or safety critical. Successful development of such systems requires knowledge of how to ensure that systems possess the following characteristics:

- Security and privacy,
- Interoperability,
- Reliability and dependability,
- Power and energy management,
- Safety,
- Stability and performance, and
- Human factors and usability.

These topics are best introduced early and infused throughout the CPS curriculum in coursework and projects, much as the best practice in engineering is to address these issues from the outset of system design.

Complementary Skills

The growing scale and complexity of engineering systems mean that engineers are increasingly working collaboratively with experts from multiple disciplines. "Soft" skills—in such areas as communication, flexibility, and an ability to work on teams, including multiple disciplines—are of particular importance for CPS engineering because the work is inherently interdisciplinary. The pace of change in science and engineering knowledge generally and the newness and rapid flux of CPS suggest that CPS courses and programs emphasizing learning and critical thinking, as well as specific techniques and methods, are needed.

BOX S.1
Paths for Teaching Cyber-Physical Systems

Potential perspectives and paths for teaching CPS include the following:

- *Exposure to CPS in K-12.* Incorporating some knowledge into K-12 courses in, for example, basic calculus, physics, programming, or robotics could relieve some of the pressure on an already-crowded undergraduate curriculum and would in any event help ensure that students arrive ready to embark on a CPS-focused curriculum when they begin their undergraduate studies. Existing science, technology, engineering, and mathematics (STEM) initiatives and the Computer Science for All initiative launched in 2016 could be used as opportunities to incorporate CPS knowledge in K-12 programs across the United States, exposing students to core concepts.
- *Vocational and community college programs.* These programs play several roles in developing the workforce: a pathway to 4-year institutions, vocational training, and updating the skills of the existing workforce. Adding CPS skills to community college programs would not only create paths to 4-year CPS degrees but would also train the workforce that will be needed to operate and maintain increasingly complex CPS. Mid-career engineers may also need to bolster their skills and knowledge as their jobs increasingly involve CPS.
- *Inclusion of CPS in introductory engineering and computer science courses.* The majority of engineers will need a basic understanding in the complexities of building and maintaining CPS.

PATHS TO CPS KNOWLEDGE

There will be multiple paths for attaining CPS knowledge and skills (Box S.1). One reason is that the workforce is likely to include both domain experts who are knowledgeable about CPS principles and a new type of engineer who is an expert at the intersection of cyber and physical issues. Another reason is that many different approaches will be undertaken at colleges and universities depending on their present circumstances, such as existing department structures and curricula, faculty expertise, and available resources.

Designing a CPS degree is quite complex and involves, for example, a careful balancing of physical and cyber aspects and general CPS and application knowledge. Because CPS degree curricula are in their infancy, they will doubtless evolve substantially as CPS are more widely deployed. Moreover, CPS programs will doubtless share with most engi-

---

- *One or more CPS survey courses taught at the undergraduate level.* Survey courses provide students with a basic understanding of CPS and the key challenges to their design, both of which are especially important for domain experts from the individual engineering disciplines (i.e., aerospace, civil, and mechanical engineering).
- *Engineering programs that include a CPS concentration or focus.* Although several engineering fields, such as mechanical and aerospace engineering, have begun incorporating some CPS principles, they may also benefit from a stronger, more deliberate approach to teaching CPS foundations; moreover, this may also be true of other areas, including civil, chemical, and biomedical engineering.
- *A (new) bachelor's-level CPS engineering degree.* The committee believes that the creation of a new type of engineer—a CPS engineer who is an expert at the intersection of the cyber and physical issues—will be needed to meet workforce needs.
- *A master's-level CPS degree.* A handful of graduate degree programs that focus on embedded systems or CPS exist, chiefly with an electrical engineering or computer science slant. An M.Sc. program aimed at graduates from other engineering fields, such as mechanical or civil engineering, would also be valuable.
- *Ph.D. programs in CPS.* The educational content in master's-level programs may suffice for some or all of the training of future faculty, but demand for CPS faculty, combined with industry demand for Ph.D. training and sustained research funding, is likely to spur institutions to establish Ph.D. programs. If CPS follows the pattern of other engineering disciplines, Ph.D.-level engineers will fill important technical leadership roles in industry, and more Ph.D.'s will take jobs in industry than will pursue academic careers.

neering degree programs the challenge of prioritizing topics to fit in a manageable 4-year program of study.

> **FINDING 3.1:** The diversity of current departmental structures, faculty expertise and interests, and curricula suggest that there are multiple feasible and appropriate models for strengthening CPS engineering. The committee envisions that universities will (1) enrich current engineering programs with CPS content, (2) create CPS survey courses, (3) create new master's-level CPS degrees, and, ultimately, (4) develop new undergraduate CPS engineering degree programs.

Many universities may not currently have the expertise or resources to establish extensive CPS education programs. A useful alternative in these cases would be to forge more limited partnerships among several departments to implement jointly taught courses. For example, key CPS content could be introduced into mechatronics, robotics, or transportation courses. Doing so over time could help reduce the burdens associated with infusing CPS throughout engineering and building the courses needed to implement a CPS program.

> **FINDING 3.2:** Because CPS engineering centers on the interaction of physical and cyber aspects of systems, it will often not be sufficient to create CPS curricula by simply combining material from existing courses. New courses will need to be designed.

> **RECOMMENDATION 3.1:** The National Science Foundation should support the development of university education programs that define a path and plan for the creation of a cyber-physical systems engineering degree.

> **RECOMMENDATION 3.2:** The National Science Foundation, professional societies, and university administrations should support and consider allocating resources for the development of new cyber-physical systems (CPS)-focused courses within existing engineering programs, new CPS-specific classes for CPS engineering majors and minors, and an overall curriculum for an undergraduate CPS engineering degree program.

> **RECOMMENDATION 3.3:** Universities should consider adding cyber-physical systems content to freshman-level introductory courses for students in all areas of engineering and computer science.

RECOMMENDATION 3.4: Engineering schools, by-and-large, have already redesigned their curricula to emphasize project-based learning. Because this is especially important for cyber-physical systems (CPS) education, these project-based courses should be extended to support CPS principles and foundations.

OPPORTUNITIES AND OBSTACLES FOR INSTITUTIONALIZING CPS CURRICULA

Several obstacles stand in the way of building successful CPS programs. The nature of CPS makes it difficult to develop and teach CPS-focused curricula. Moreover, although students may be interested in CPS technologies or in the applications that CPS enable, they may not realize that they ought to seek out courses or a program that emphasizes CPS knowledge and skills. Also, few mechanisms exist to support extensive faculty commitment to a new interdisciplinary discipline, which makes it hard to develop, recruit, or retain the faculty needed to provide an up-to-date CPS education for undergraduate students. Moreover, an array of resources—from new textbooks to laboratory equipment—is needed to support any new curriculum.

Drawing Students to CPS

At the undergraduate level, one key will be exposing STEM-oriented students to the existence of the field of CPS, its links to related areas like robotics and the Internet of Things (IoT), and the potential benefits of its formal study. One important opportunity is to include CPS as part of freshman "introduction to engineering" programs across engineering and not just in computer science and electrical engineering.

FINDING 4.1: Although there are many STEM courses and programs at the high school and undergraduate level that introduce the students to some CPS elements, such programs often do not provide a broad introduction to CPS foundations and principles and tend to be overly focused either on simplistic applications or discipline-centric content.

RECOMMENDATION 4.1: Those developing K-12 science, technology, engineering, and mathematics (STEM) programs and educating and training STEM teachers should consider opportunities to enrich these programs with cyber-physical systems (CPS) concepts and applications in order to lay intellectual foundations for future work and expose students to CPS career opportunities.

FINDING 4.2: Incoming college students appear to be unfamiliar with the term CPS, CPS concepts, and job opportunities in CPS. They are, however, drawn to courses and programs in more widely visible CPS-related topics such as robotics, the Internet of Things (IoT), health care, smart cities, and the Industrial Internet.

RECOMMENDATION 4.2: Those developing cyber-physical systems engineering courses and programs should consider leveraging the visibility of and student interest in areas such as robotics, the Internet of Things, health care, smart cities, and the Industrial Internet in descriptions of careers, courses, and programs and when selecting applications used in courses and projects.

Recruiting, Retaining, and Developing the Needed Faculty

Faculty teaching CPS courses will be most effective if they are able to draw on expertise in particular aspects of CPS, knowledge of the other aspects of a complete CPS system, and domain- or application-specific needs. Today, most CPS education (and research) is being performed by a small number of faculty members who previously established themselves in a related field and then ventured into this newer, more interdisciplinary field.

In the long term, academic institutions will have opportunities to recruit new faculty who have graduated with a CPS degree or specialization and who have a record of conducting CPS-specific research as well as people with industrial experience with CPS engineering. Indeed, some institutions have already begun explicitly looking for such individuals. Both research funding and opportunities for academic advancement are needed to develop a pool of faculty. The National Science Foundation's Cyber-Physical Systems program has helped build an academic community around CPS and foster links between academia and industry. The parallel development of several well-recognized CPS conferences and the creation of a new CPS journal have also made it easier for faculty with a multidisciplinary profile to establish themselves as CPS researchers and still meet the academic evaluation criteria. Nevertheless, it will take time and investment to build the necessary complement of faculty to educate those who engineer CPS.

FINDING 4.3: Because CPS is a new field that draws on multiple disciplines, not all institutions can be expected to have enough faculty with the requisite knowledge to teach all of the courses needed for a CPS degree program.

RECOMMENDATION 4.3: The National Science Foundation should support the development of cyber-physical systems faculty through the use of teaching grants and fellowships.

Despite the challenges of entering a new field, young faculty may have an advantage becoming leaders in the CPS field, given the novelty of the area, because they do not need to compete with the large number of well-established and well-recognized leaders found in more mature fields.

Developing Needed Courses and Instructional Materials

Although the committee was encouraged by the release of several textbooks during the course of its work, the number of textbooks, curricular materials, and laboratory facilities that exist to support CPS remains limited. Just as merely regrouping current classes will not yield a CPS curriculum, current texts may not fully incorporate the effects of the physical system on cyber technology, and vice versa. Furthermore, often the complexity of CPS demands that students gain a full understanding of how the physical environment impacts these systems. Realistic models can provide some of this knowledge, but testbeds will be needed for students to fully realize the constraints the physical environment can create. These testbeds are expensive to create and maintain, and many universities do not have, or will not allocate, the resources to create such testbeds.

FINDING 4.4: If they are to teach new CPS courses and build CPS programs, universities will need to allocate time and resources to develop CPS course materials and to provide the necessary laboratory space and equipment (including both virtual and physical testbeds).

FINDING 4.5: Testbeds are needed to provide students with sufficiently realistic applications and problems. These can be both virtual and physical and can be remotely accessed and shared among multiple institutions and developed and operated in cooperation with industry.

RECOMMENDATION 4.4: The National Science Foundation, professional societies, and universities should support the development and evolution of cyber-physical systems textbooks, class modules (including laboratory modules), and testbeds. These parties should partner with industry in developing and maintaining realistic testbeds.

* * *

As CPS become more pervasive, demand will grow for a workforce with the capacity and capability to design, develop, and maintain them. An understanding of not only the cyber or the physical aspects of systems, but also their interactions will become more and more valuable. A workforce with these skills will be better positioned to help industry pursue current and future advances across the myriad applications for CPS. The actions recommended in this report point to ways to ensure that aspiring engineers and computer scientists are equipped with the skills necessary to meet the demand for a modern CPS workforce.

1

The Transformative Nature of CPS and Workforce Needs

This chapter discusses the transformative nature of cyber-physical systems (CPS), their importance to industry, and the associated workforce needs. It looks at broad indicators of the economic importance of CPS applications as well as testimony presented to the committee about the CPS skills sought by industry.

THE TRANSFORMATIVE NATURE OF CPS

The engineered world has seen a major transformation during the last few decades. Elements that previously existed in purely mechanical or electrical (i.e., physical) form, and in particular those elements describing logic, control, and decision-making, increasingly take the form of embedded systems and software (i.e., cyber elements). The acronym CPS is often used to describe "engineered systems that are built from, and depend upon, the seamless integration of computational algorithms and physical components."[1] In this definition, "cyber" refers to the computers, software, data structures, and networks that support decision-making within the system, and "physical" denotes not only the parts of the physical systems (e.g., the mechanical and electrical components of an automated vehicle) but also the physical world in which the system interacts (e.g.,

---

[1] Definition from National Science Foundation (NSF), 2016, "Cyber-Physical Systems," program solicitation 16-549, NSF document number nsf16549, March 4, https://www.nsf.gov/publications/pub_summ.jsp?ods_key=nsf16549.

roads and pedestrians). CPS is closely related to terms in common use today, such as Internet of Things (IoT), the Industrial Internet, and smart cities, and to the fields of robotics and systems engineering (Box 1.1).

Several emerging technology trends support the increased deployment of CPS:

- Communication networks, databases, and distributed systems allow control and decision-making on physical systems to be done remotely, collaboratively, and in a distributed manner, which is enabling functionality impossible a few years ago.
- The developments that have given rise to the field of data science make it possible to collect, store, analyze, and act on large amount of real-world data.
- Decreasing costs of components and systems have allowed the use of CPS within everyday devices such as home thermostats and automobile brakes. For example, lower cost sensors are being deployed across the board, from the use of sensor nets to detect approaching natural disasters such as flooding and earthquakes to those that support safer car travel.
- Wide deployment and increased reliability of high-speed wireless networks support devices that rely on a continuous connection to the Internet.

CPS can be small and self-contained, such as an artificial pancreas, or very large and complex, such as a regional energy grid. They are increasingly used to provide economically or societally important capabilities, many with critical infrastructure or life-safety implications (Box 1.2). CPS can provide extraordinary flexibility by allowing unprecedented growth in economy, functionality, safety, performance, and accuracy of control and operational decision-making. Indeed, virtually all industries have embraced CPS. A recent McKinsey Global Institute report on the IoT, for which CPS provides the technical foundation, captured some of the economic importance of CPS applications succinctly by stating, "the hype has been great—the value may be greater."[2] The McKinsey report estimates a potential worldwide economic impact of as much as "$11.1 trillion per year in 2025 for IoT applications in nine settings"—devices attached to or inside the human body, homes, retail environments, offices, factories, custom production environments, vehicles, cities, and other outside settings.[3] Gartner recently forecast a 30 percent increase in the number of

---

[2] McKinsey Global Institute, 2015, *The Internet of Things: Mapping the Value Beyond the Hype*, June, http://www.mckinsey.com/business-functions/business-technology/our-insights/the-internet-of-things-the-value-of-digitizing-the-physical-world.

[3] Ibid, p. 2-3.

BOX 1.1
Areas Related to Cyber-Physical Systems

The field of cyber-physical systems (CPS) is closely related to other fields and underpins several important technical visions.

- *Robotics* focuses on systems incorporating sensors and actuators that operate autonomously or semi-autonomously in cooperation with humans.[1] It encompasses an array of topics that include kinematics, dynamics, and path planning; robot hardware and control software; perception, sensing, and state estimation; and control of manipulators and vehicles. Many robots would be considered CPS, and the field of robotics draws on many CPS principles. At the same time, many CPS are not robots, and some of the topics covered in a robotics program are particular to that field.
- *Systems engineering*, a field that focuses on the design and management of complex systems, also contributes significantly to CPS, and in particular to such topics as modeling and integration. However, systems engineering typically concentrates on the organization, management, and integration required for large systems but does not necessarily address the detailed technological needs that arise in combining the physical with the cyber aspects of systems.
- The *Internet of Things* (IoT) is defined as "a dynamic global network infrastructure with self-configuring capabilities based on standard and interoperable communication protocols where physical and virtual 'things' have identities, physical attributes, and virtual personalities and use intelligent interfaces, and are seamlessly integrated into the information network, and often communicate data associated with users and their environments."[2] As IoT progresses, it is increasingly being applied to applications that require CPS characteristics such as control, real-time response, and safety-critical operation. IoT applications like smart cities (see below) are rapidly becoming more sophisticated and reliant on CPS capabilities.
- The *Industrial Internet*[3] combines the IoT with the ability to collect and analyze large volumes of data to manage industrial systems and operations.
- *Smart cities* is a vision in which urban areas and other communities leverage information technology to better manage community infrastructure and resources, improve efficiency, and enhance the quality of life. As smart city applications augment sensing and monitoring with real-time response and control, they become reliant on CPS capabilities.

---

[1] Institute of Electrical and Electronics Engineers, UAE Section homepage, http://www.ieee-uae.com/?page_id=267.

[2] Ian Smith, ed., 2012, *The Internet of Things 2012: New Horizons*, Internet of Things European Research Cluster, Platinum, Halifax, U.K.

[3] The term "Industrial Internet" was coined at GE (see J. Leber, 2012, "General Electric Pitches an Industrial Internet," *MIT Technology Review*, November 28, https://www.technologyreview.com/s/507831/general-electric-pitches-an-industrial-internet/) but is now used more widely, including by the Industrial Internet Consortium, which was co-founded by GE.

> **BOX 1.2**
> **A CPS-Enabled Future**
>
> Cyber-physical systems (CPS) can be used to provide economically or societally important capabilities in the following areas:
>
> - *Transportation.* CPS is already used in automobiles that can sense impending crashes and perform various tasks to protect passengers. CPS technologies promise to greatly reduce the annual death toll from car crashes caused by human error and to reduce greatly the time wasted and pollution generated by highway congestion. CPS technologies for aviation and airport safety technology could relieve congestion and enable safe integration of autonomous air vehicles into U.S. airspace.
> - *Manufacturing.* The complexity of what can be designed and built and what society demands is constantly increasing. The time scale for product development cycles is decreasing, even as product variety is increasing. CPS technologies could enhance both product design (e.g., by defining more functionality through software) and manufacturing (e.g., by enabling more capable or efficient manufacturing facilities).
> - *Health care.* CPS are found in today's medical devices that can sense glucose levels or heart rhythm abnormalities and intervene to restore normal body function Applied more broadly, CPS will help to scale access to care for a growing aging population. CPS formal specification and verification techniques could help in the design of more cost-effective, easier-to-certify, and safer medical products.
> - *Energy.* Renewable electric energy resources are intermittent and uncertain, necessitating new sensors, switches, and meters, and also an infrastructure for realizing an adaptive, secure, resilient, efficient, and cost-effective electricity distribution system that allows consumers to manage their energy use.
> - *Agriculture.* With global population projected to surpass 9 billion people by 2050, an uncertain and changing climate future, and up to one third of food lost between production and consumption,[1] systems that generate food, fiber, feed, and biofuels need to be more efficient. CPS technologies could increase sustainability and efficiency (less waste) throughout the value chain.
>
> ---
> [1] Food and Agriculture Organization, 2011, *Global Food Losses and Food Waste*, Rome, Italy, http://www.fao.org/food-loss-and-food-waste/en/, p. v.

"connected things" from 2015 to 2016 and a threefold increase to over 20 billion devices in 2020.[4] A related concept is the Industrial Internet, which combines IoT and big data analytics for industrial applications. A 2015 report from GE and the consulting firm Accenture cites projections

---

[4] Gartner, Inc., 2015, "Gartner Says 6.4 Billion Connected 'Things' Will Be in Use in 2016, Up 30 Percent From 2015," press release, November 10, 2015, http://www.gartner.com/newsroom/id/3165317.

that worldwide Industrial Internet spending could reach $500 million by 2020 and be responsible for as much as $15 trillion of the global economy by 2030.[5] At the same time, firms in the information technology sector are increasingly investing in CPS areas such as self-driving cars (e.g., Google and Uber) and the IoT (e.g., IBM).

Speaking to the potential of CPS and the technical challenges of realizing that potential, in testimony to the House Committee on Science and Technology in 2008, Don Winter, vice president for engineering and information technology at Boeing Phantom Works, observed the following:

> Cyber-physical systems are pervasive at Boeing, and in the aerospace industry at large. They are becoming increasingly prevalent in other sectors, notably automotive and energy management. Their importance to our products is huge and their complexity is growing at an exponential rate.[6]

The contribution of CPS to aerospace systems has grown dramatically, noted Winter, having risen from less than 10 percent of the design, development, validation, and certification cost for transport aircraft in the 1970s to about 50 percent by the 2000s.

It is worth observing that even as it offers enormous safety benefits, the adoption of CPS also introduces new risks. For example, although it is also susceptible to failure, a purely mechanical linkage may be less dangerous than separate sensors and actuators that could lead to failure and injury as a result of a software mistake, hardware malfunction, or cybersecurity attack. These risks magnify the need for a highly skilled workforce.

Foundational advances resulting from academic research will support the next generation of CPS that can be designed, implemented, deployed, and maintained to meet requirements using emerging functional and nonfunctional properties. Advances in achieving functional properties allow new solutions to be realized; for example, tomorrow's solutions will allow micro-electric grid transactions for higher energy efficiency and disease prevention (not just maintenance). Advances in achieving nonfunctional properties (i.e., security, safety, reliability, and dependability) will enable future systems to operate with increased confidence in the presence of risk—for example, realizing confidence in city-scale autonomous transportation systems.

---

[5] General Electric and Accenture, 2014, *Industrial Internet Insights Report for 2015*, http://www.ge.com/digital/sites/default/files/industrial-internet-insights-report.pdf, accessed November 1, 2016.

[6] Don C. Winter, 2008, Testimony at a hearing on the Networking and Information Technology Research and Development (NITRD) Program, Committee on Science and Technology, U.S. House of Representatives, July 31.

The National Science Foundation (NSF) has an ongoing CPS research program that was given additional impetus by recommendations of August 2007 and December 2010 reports of the President's Council of Advisors on Science and Technology.[7] Reflective of both the diverse applications of CPS and its importance for progress in many sectors, the NSF program works with a wide array of federal mission agencies: the U.S. Department of Homeland Security's Science and Technology Directorate; the U.S. Department of Transportation's Federal Highway Administration and Intelligent Transportation Systems Joint Program Office; the National Aeronautics and Space Administration's Aeronautics Research Mission Directorate (ARMD); several institutes and centers of the National Institutes of Health; and the U.S. Department of Agriculture's National Institute of Food and Agriculture.[8]

The National Institute of Standards and Technology has established a Cyber-Physical Systems and Smart Grid Program Office pursuing research and the development of architectures, frameworks, and standards for CPS and CPS applications.[9] Other federal CPS research initiatives include the Defense Advanced Research Projects Agency's Adaptive Vehicle Make and High-Assurance Cyber Military Systems programs and the Department of Transportation's Connected Vehicle and Intelligent Transportation Systems program. CPS research initiatives can also be found in many other countries (Box 1.3).

BUILDING A CPS WORKFORCE

It proved difficult for the committee to obtain comprehensive data on demand for CPS skills and knowledge. It is especially challenging to gather systematic information of the sort requested for an emerging, highly interdisciplinary field like CPS. It is likewise difficult to gather even anecdotal information from smaller firms because they tend not to have readily identifiable points of contact on these issues. No surveys appear to have been conducted on industrial demand for skills or of CPS-related university programs in the United States. Nor do current

---

[7] From the President's Council of Advisors on Science and Technology reports *Leadership Under Challenge: Information Technology R&D in a Competitive World: An Assessment of the Federal Networking and Information Technology R&D Program*, August 2007, and *Designing a Digital Future: Federally Funded Research and Development in Networking and Information Technology*, December 2010, https://www.whitehouse.gov/administration/eop/ostp/pcast/docsreports; and NSF, 2016, "Cyber-Physical Systems," program solicitation 16-549.

[8] NSF, "Cyber-Physical Systems (CPS)," https://www.nsf.gov/funding/pgm_summ.jsp?pims_id=503286, accessed November 1, 2016.

[9] National Institute of Standards and Technology, "Cyber-Physical Systems," https://www.nist.gov/el/cyber-physical-systems, accessed November 1, 2016.

> **BOX 1.3**
> **Global Investments in CPS Research**
>
> The following are examples of long-term research initiatives in cyber-physical systems (CPS):
>
> - *Germany's Industry 4.0* program seeks to use the potential of cyber-physical systems (the Internet of Things) to maintain industrial leadership. Industry 4.0 thus covers manufacturing, services, and industrial design. One focus is on intelligent production systems and processes and the realization of distributed and networked production sites.[1]
> - The *European Union* (EU) initiated a major joint technology initiative with public-private funding—with around $7 billion in proposed spending on embedded systems and CPS by 2013[2]—by European nations and industry called Advanced Research and Technology for Embedded Intelligence Systems[3] and subsequently merged with an integrated circuit technology initiative to create the European Technology Platform on Smart Systems Integration (EPoSS), which identifies research and development needs and policies that would foster smart system integration.[4] The current EU Framework Programme for Research and Innovation (Horizon 2020) includes a research program on smart CPS as well as programs in related areas, such as smart systems, autonomous systems, intelligent transport systems, factory automation, the Internet of Things, and smart communities.
> - *South Korea* is pursuing related initiatives through various Korean National IT Industry Promotion Agency (NIPA) programs. CPS was also a major point of discussion during a high-level Information and Communication Technology Policy Forum in late 2015.[5]
>
> ---
>
> [1] EU-Japan Center for Industrial Cooperation, 2015, *Digital Economy In Japan and the EU: An Assessment of the Common Challenges and the Collaboration Potential*, Tokyo, Japan, March.
> [2] National Institute of Standards and Technology, 2013, *Strategic R&D Opportunities for 21st Century Cyber-Physical Systems: Connecting Computer and Information Systems with the Physical World*, Gaithersburg, Md., January.
> [3] IEEE Control Systems Society, 2011, *The Impact of Control Technology* (T. Samad and A.M. Annaswamy, eds.), http://www.ieeecss.org.
> [4] SUPA KT, "High Level Strategic Research and Innovation Agenda of the ICT Components and Systems Industries as represented by ARTEMIS, ENIAC and EPoSS (2012)," http://kt.supa.ac.uk/market/artemis-eniac-eposs.
> [5] U.S. Embassy in Seoul, Korea.

government statistics provide sufficient granularity to separate out CPS positions from other computing or engineering jobs. The committee was not in a position to commission systematic surveys of either industry or academia to collect such information itself.

Lacking comprehensive data about workforce needs in CPS, the committee relied on the perspectives of industry experts who participated in

> **BOX 1.4**
> **Comments on Industry Need for a CPS-Capable Workforce**
>
> Workshop participants and briefers to the committee from several industry sectors provided many comments about the growing importance of CPS in industry and the resulting demand for CPS skills. These included the following:
>
> - *Automotive industry.* Describing why demand for CPS talent is growing in the automotive industry, Craig Stephens, from Ford Research and Advanced Engineering, noted that although basic automobile engineering knowledge (such as power train, combustion, and emissions) remains fundamental, automotive engineers also need to be able to design, develop, and test systems that include communication and sensing technologies and more sophisticated computer controls. These new skills are especially important in new applications, such as electrification, vehicle-to-vehicle communication, active safety features, and automated or autonomous driving. Stephens noted that the auto industry has been successful in providing the necessary training, but companies like Ford hope that employees will enter one day with a stronger foundation in CPS. Dan Johnson, Honeywell, Inc., cited aeronautics and aerospace as another transportation industry in which CPS play an increasingly important role. For example, numerous CPS-intensive systems (e.g., aircraft, airports, air traffic control, maintenance, and passenger services) make up the air transportation environment.
> - *Agriculture and construction equipment.* Jon Williams, a system architect at John Deere, observed that the agricultural and construction equipment sector is increasingly CPS-intensive as well. For example, Deere manufactures partial and fully autonomous vehicles, provides mesh wireless and telematics links between vehicles, updates and diagnoses faults in its products remotely, and is developing applications for the agronomic data that its products collect. Moreover, Williams noted, a large industrial farm today is a system of systems and requires a systems approach to developing and deploying products and services rather than the traditional focus on individual products.

the two workshops convened during its study as well as a set of briefings. A list of all workshop speakers or briefers to the committee, which included a number from industry, can be found in Appendix B.

Workshop speakers representing a wide array of industry sectors—automotive, agriculture, medical devices, and space, along with a large industrial conglomerate and a vendor of CPS engineering software tools, discussed the changing nature of their products, the array of new skills needed in their engineering workforce, and the challenges they face in developing the necessary talent. A summary of some of their observations is provided in Box 1.4. People from diverse industry sectors reported that they needed people with CPS engineering skills. In some cases, products

- *Medical devices.* Scott Hareland, from the medical devices firm Medtronic, discussed the increasing capability of medical devices to monitor and diagnose health conditions, be life-sustaining (pacemakers), or simply improve life through pain reduction. He observed that today's engineers are not equipped with all of the skills needed to develop future medical devices.
- *Space.* David Nichols and Daniel Dvorak described the CPS needs of the Jet Propulsion Laboratory (JPL), which designs, builds, deploys, and operates spacecraft systems such as the Mars Science Laboratory's rover *Curiosity* and the Cassini orbiter. Jobs at JPL that require CPS skills include mission formulation dealing with autonomy requirements; engineering design at the assembly, subsystem, and system levels; design activities specifically related to autonomous control (fault management, verification and validation, and mission operations); systems engineering at all levels; and mission, software, and safety assurance. JPL tends to "grow" flight project engineers internally because it finds it hard to find graduates who already possess all the needed CPS and other engineering skills. Indeed, about four-fifths of JPL's science and engineering new hires are recent graduates that JPL intends to develop through hands-on project work and mentoring from senior engineers.
- *Tools supporting CPS development.* John Mills, from SimuQuest, a software company that develops products that support model-based system engineering, identified key knowledge areas that he is looking for in employees: plant modeling, algorithm design, control system design, network understanding, and engineering process. There is also a new emphasis on CPS skills, including nondeterminism, managing timing and latency, and co-simulation. Mills noted that while Ford, GE, and Deere may have the resources to train their employees in CPS skills, a smaller company like SimuQuest has a harder time doing so.

SOURCE: Adapted from National Research Council, 2015, *Interim Report on 21st Century Cyber-Physical Systems Education*, The National Academies Press, Washington, D.C., doi:10.17226/21762.

were not being developed because there were not enough people available with the CPS skills necessary to do the job. In other cases, people from industry noted that their workforce would be restructured if more CPS-educated individuals were available.

Speaking to the demand for CPS skills, Joseph Salvo, director at GE Global Research observed that "going forward . . . almost all of our employees are going to be touched by this." Asked how many CPS engineers Ford Motor Company needed, Craig Stephens, from Ford's Research and Advanced Engineering organization, responded "[the] short answer is, more than we can get."

Given the prevalence of CPS throughout industry, the work of many engineers revolves around CPS, whether they consider themselves experts in this area or not. Many have not received formal education or training in key CPS topics, such as formal methods, verification, or security, and may not fully understand the challenges of designing the software or physical systems for life-critical systems.

Ad hoc CPS system design and implementation runs the risk of not supporting the scalability, security, and design flexibility required to meet today's and tomorrow's needs. This is of particular concern given the role CPS plays in mission- and safety-critical systems, and the cybersecurity challenges faced with all computer systems. Better education and training and the development of a CPS discipline is therefore a priority, since many if not most of the systems that society relies on will be CPS.

Developing effective CPS solutions requires a workforce that has the right mix training and skills. This workforce will include skill levels ranging from those who can help develop sophisticated capabilities to those who can help deploy and maintain CPS solutions over long periods of time. Engineering projects are by nature collaborative, and engineering teams involve a range of expertise, including CPS.

Accordingly, a variety of educational and training regimes will be needed. The multidisciplinary skills required will build on existing workforce capabilities in areas of engineering, computer science, and information technology. To that end, part of the effort will need to focus on supplementing the skills of the existing workforce, while another part will need to focus on a future workforce that has all prerequisite skills built in from their education.

FINDING 1.1: CPS are emerging as an area of engineering with significant economical and societal implications. Major industrial sectors such as transportation, medicine, energy, defense, and information technology increasingly need a workforce capable of designing and engineering products and services that intimately combine cyber elements (computing hardware and software) and physical components and manage their interactions and impact on the physical environment). Although it is difficult to quantify the demand, a likely implication is that more CPS-capable engineers will be needed.

CPS: AN EMERGING ENGINEERING DISCIPLINE

The emergence of a new field such as CPS from preexisting domains of knowledge is not a new occurrence. In fact, analogies can be drawn to the history of computer and software engineering. Electrical engineers in the 1940s could not have conceived of computers as commodities. Then, a computer was a very large room packed with rack after rack of hot vacuum tube assemblies, relays, huge power supplies, and the unenviable punched card reader and line printer. The field of computer engineering slowly emerged as a separate discipline and practice. The separate discipline and practice of software engineering later answered the need for people to more easily and effectively program the computers. It should come as no surprise that, much the same way that an army of electrical engineers is no longer required to build a computer, there is no longer the need for armies of varied engineering disciplines required to build, program, and employ small processors with sensors and controllers (either attached or built in) as components in other systems—or, for that matter, as systems themselves. However, although the components and tools for designing small, embedded systems are accessible to a hobbyist, the skills and knowledge necessary to develop a large system with verifiable reliability and safety requirements are considerable.

Following a similar pattern, CPS incorporate components of disciplines such as embedded systems, software engineering, control systems, networking, and systems engineering. In fact, domains such as aerospace and mechanical engineering and related fields such as robotics have incorporated many CPS principles for some time. The experts in this nascent field will be experts on this intersection of disciplines.

FINDING 1.2: The future CPS workforce is likely to include a combination of (1) engineers trained in foundational fields (such as electrical and computing engineering, mechanical engineering, systems engineering, and computer science); (2) engineers trained in specific applied engineering fields (such as aerospace and civil engineering); and (3) CPS engineers, who focus on the knowledge and skills spanning cyber technology and physical systems that operate in the physical world.

FINDING 1.3: Given that most entry-level engineering and computer science positions are filled by undergraduates, it is important to incorporate CPS into the undergraduate engineering and computer science curricula.

RECOMMENDATION 1.1: The National Science Foundation, together with universities, should support the creation and evolution of undergraduate education courses, programs, and pathways so that engineering and computer science graduates have more opportunities to gain the knowledge and skills required to engineer cyber-physical systems. The efforts should be complemented by initiatives to augment the skills of the existing workforce through continuing education and master's degree programs.

2

CPS Principles, Foundations, System Characteristics, and Complementary Skills

This chapter examines at a high level the knowledge required to engineer cyber-physical systems (CPS). It draws on an examination of existing courses, programs, and instructional materials as well as consideration of the topics highlighted in comments to the committee from industry experts. Many of these foundations are also present in areas like computer science, engineering, and robotics, but the emphasis in CPS is on the integration of physical and cyber aspects. The chapter starts with a discussion of this integration and associated principles.

Drawing on these principles, this chapter identified six foundations for a CPS curriculum: basic computing concepts, computing for the physical world, discrete and continuous mathematics, cross-cutting applications, modeling, and CPS system development. The chapter turns next to a discussion of system characteristics such as scale, complexity, and safety criticality. These topics are best introduced early and infused throughout in CPS coursework and projects, much as the best practice in engineering is to address these issues from the outset of system design. The chapter closes with a discussion of complementary skills of value for CPS careers: learning to learn and critical thinking, soft skills, and entrepreneurship.

Given that the potential content for CPS is broad and evolving, the emphasis here is on general principles, foundations, system characteristics, and skills rather a large array of specific facts or techniques. This approach is especially important in light of the wide breadth of material relevant to engineering CPS and the emerging and fast-paced nature of the field. With the right foundations, students will be positioned to learn about new developments on the job.

Because engineering courses and curricula are already packed, it is not viable to simply add more material to span the physical and cyber dimensions—and certainly not to double the amount of material. Nor can all relevant topics fit into the CPS core curriculum or these principles and foundations. For example, bio-memetics, an approach that is useful in areas such as robotics, is not included. (Robotics is instead treated as an elective course in the representative curricula in Boxes 3.4 through 3.7.)

PRINCIPLES: INTEGRATING THE PHYSICAL AND CYBER

The core principle of CPS is the bridging of engineering and physical world applications and the computer engineering hardware and computer science cyber worlds. Basic principles of the physical world include elements of physics, modeling, and real-world intangibles such as uncertainty and risk. Concurrently, the principles of computer engineering and computer science worlds deal with embedded systems, networking, programming, and algorithms. CPS education thus goes beyond exposure to the traditional dynamical systems models (ordinary differential or difference equations) to an understanding of physical impacts not only at the physical layer, but also across the physical-cyber interface.

Sensors are an example of a hardware bridge between the physical and cyber worlds. They are the primary devices that collect data from the physical world that are then used as input to the cyber world. Understanding the properties and principles of sensors and how to use them in a manner that is aware of sensor and real-world constraints is critical. Unfortunately, high-level abstractions used to simplify system development often have the undesirable side effect of hiding key physical world principles that programmers need to know if the CPS they develop are to work properly. Once raw data are collected, they are processed via signal processing techniques. The required principles of signal processing include linear signals and systems theory, analog and digital filtering, time and frequency domain analysis, convolution, linear transforms like the discrete Fourier transform and fast Fourier transform, noise and statistical characterization of signals, machine learning, and decision and sensor fusion. In CPS, considerations of the implementations of these signal processing techniques on embedded CPUs, running in real time and with safety critical implications, are necessary, as is the topic of sensor reliability. Often these issues are not considered in classical signal processing courses.

Control is a central tenet of CPS. Relevant elements of control theory include stability and optimization as well as control techniques in the context of networks, hybrid systems, stochastic systems, and digital systems. Of particular importance in the cyber domain are the implications for control of distributed systems and the inherent delays they impose.

In today's networked, wireless, and real-time world, and as cyber-physical systems become embedded in our economy and society, knowledge of the principles underlying these topics is also necessary for CPS engineering. Areas where students need this knowledge include the following:

- *Communication and networking.* CPS requires an understanding from physical-layer principles to protocols, layered architectures, and the many real-world properties of wireless communications.
- *Real time.* An understanding of topics like real-time scheduling theory, temporal semantics in programs, and clock synchronization in networks is needed.
- *Distributed systems.* The distributed and networked nature of CPS in many of the applications of interest should be included in CPS education. Even though distributed systems and networking are covered in traditional engineering or computer science curricula, these courses often do not address CPS issues. CPS combines the hardware implementation with the software that runs the algorithms, all operating in a natural world setting.
- *Embedded systems.* A strong education and training on the principles of embedded software, the many principles of programming, algorithms, software design, formal methods, and platforms (architectures and operating systems) are necessary to enable the development of reliable and high-quality cyber components of a CPS system.
- *Physical properties.* It is important to understand and be able to model the physical properties of the environments and hardware platforms. Software design principles that address the realisms of the physical world in such a way as to satisfy safety, reliability, real-time performance, risk management, and security requirements need to be part of the curriculum.
- *Human interaction.* Human factors design, human-in-the-loop control, and understanding and accounting for the behavioral responses of humans are important for many CPS. One important design issue is making CPS easy for humans to operate, control, and maintain. Similar to other engineering disciplines, hands-on projects and interdisciplinary teamwork are also fundamental to understanding and seeing core principles applied.

FINDING 2.1: Core CPS knowledge involves not only an understanding of the basics of physical engineering and cyber design and implementation, but also understanding how the physical and cyber aspects influence and affect each other.

RECOMMENDATION 2.1: Cyber-physical systems educational programs should provide a foundation that highlights the interaction of cyber and physical aspects of systems. Most current courses fail to emphasize the interaction, implying that new courses and instructional materials are needed.

Examples of curricula that highlight this interaction are provided in Chapter 3 (Boxes 3.2 to 3.7).

FOUNDATIONS OF CPS

Drawing on these principles, the committee identified six key overarching foundations for a CPS curriculum (Box 2.1).

• Foundation 1, *basic computing concepts,* is included to emphasize that the cyber expertise required cannot be achieved with only one or two programming classes; it can only be attained with solid training in computing that draws on examples and case studies from the physical domain. In particular, it is necessary to teach how the properties of the

---

**BOX 2.1
Foundations of Cyber-Physical Systems**

Foundation 1. Basic Computing Concepts

The cyber expertise required for cyber-physical systems (CPS) cannot be achieved with only one or two programming classes; it can only be attained with solid training in computing. The basic computing concepts listed below should be taught using examples and case studies from the physical domain. These concepts are as follows:

- Embedded hardware;
- Data structures and algorithms;
- Models of computation, including automata theory (relevant to the finite state machines widely used in CPS) and discrete event systems;
- Programming;
- Software engineering and model-based design; and
- Real-time operating systems and programming for networks.

continued

BOX 2.1 Continued

Foundation 2. Computing for the Physical World

There is a need for computing foundations to embrace physical world properties and constraints. Real-world complexities often give rise to situations not addressed by the software and often result in failures. Software designs and implementations must be aware of the resource limitations of the platforms themselves as well as conditions that the real world imposes on the platform. Students will need to understand are the following concepts:

- Properties of sensors and analysis of signals;
- Programming with sensors and actuators in open environments and with multiple modalities;
- Real-time embedded systems;
- Resource management and constraints such as time, memory size, and power; and
- Techniques such as redundancy and fault-tolerance for managing unreliability in physical systems.

Foundation 3. Discrete and Continuous Mathematics

Both discrete and continuous mathematics are needed as foundational skills for all CPS engineers. This reflects the critical fact that CPS deals with both continuous and discrete systems and having the knowledge to deal with that integration is critical. Concepts students will need to understand are as follows:

- Graph theory and combinatorics;
- Probability, statistics, and stochastic processes;
- Logic;
- Linear algebra; and
- Calculus and differential equations.

Foundation 4. Cross-cutting Application of Sensing, Actuation, Control, Communication, and Computing

This foundation is essential due to the cross-cutting focus of CPS between the physical and cyber aspects of systems, as well as control over communication networks and sensing, signal processing, and actuation with real-time constraints. The topic needs to permeate all aspects of the curriculum. Knowledge of control, signal processing, and embedded software design and implementation are at the core of this foundational principle. Concepts will include the following:

- Control principles including linear and nonlinear systems, stochastic systems, adaptive control, system identification, hybrid control;
- Optimization and optimal control of dynamic systems;

- Networking concepts including wireless communications, synchronous and asynchronous communications, and ad-hoc networking;
- Real-time analysis including task models describing real-world information sources, time-triggered or event-triggered control, decision-making with noisy data;
- Signal processing using control, computation, and communication models;
- Safety, reliability, and dependability;
- Security and privacy;
- Impact of physical properties on software requirements;
- Human factors related to human-in-loop and behavioral aspects; and
- Networked control.

Foundation 5. Modeling of Heterogeneous and Dynamic Systems Integrating Control, Computing, and Communication

CPS modeling requires a complete picture of control, communications, and computing with emphasis on representing and accounts for modularity, abstraction, uncertainty, and heterogeneity. Relevant techniques include linear and nonlinear models, stochastic models, and discrete-event and hybrid models, and associated design methodologies based on optimization, probability theory, and dynamic programming are needed. Key concepts include the following:

- Properties of the physical world, including uncertainty and risk;
- Properties of computational devices, including computational and power limits;
- Properties of communication systems, including limitations of wireless communications;
- Error detection and correction;
- Merging physical and computational modeling; and
- Commonalities between signals and systems and finite-state automata.

Foundation 6. CPS System Development

CPS development, from initial requirements to certification with emphasis on safety-critical systems, high confidence, and resiliency, requires a life cycle view. Key concepts that transcend the entire life cycle are as follows:

- Safety, resilience, security, and privacy;
- Requirement development;
- Assurance cases and hazard analysis;
- Formal verification and validation;
- Model-based design and tools;
- System design, including design for system evolution and life-cycle certification;
- Platforms such as the Internet of Things or cloud computing; and
- Testing CPS in the laboratory and in their intended environment.

physical world have to be addressed in the cyber world to achieve the system characteristics listed in the next subsection.

- Foundation 2, *computing for the physical world*, highlights the need to include properties and constraints of the physical world. Real-world complexities often give rise to situations not addressed by the software, often resulting in failures; consequently, it is necessary to have a foundation in laws of the physical world. Software designs and implementations need to take into account the resource limitations of the platforms themselves as well as conditions that the real world imposes on the platform.
- Foundation 3, *discrete and continuous mathematics*, highlights advanced math beyond calculus needed for CPS engineering. This reflects the fact that CPS deals with both continuous and discrete systems, and the knowledge on how to deal with that integration is critical.
- Foundation 4, *cross-cutting application of sensing, actuation, control, communication, and computing* encompasses knowledge of control, signal processing, and embedded software design and implementation that one would expect to permeate all aspects of the curriculum
- Foundation 5, stresses the need for *modeling of heterogeneous and dynamic systems integrating control, computing, and communication* with an emphasis on uncertainty and heterogeneity. Such work is especially challenging because physical and cyber modeling use different and often incompatible models. Focusing on the merging and interactions of models across the physical and cyber aspects of systems is necessary.
- Foundation 6, *CPS system development* identifies the requirements for a life-cycle view of developing a CPS from initial requirements to certification to deployment. Concepts that transcend the entire life cycle include safety, resilience, security, and privacy.

SYSTEM CHARACTERISTICS

Building systems that operate with increased confidence in the presence of uncertainty and with acceptable levels of risk requires an understanding of how to address relevant design aspects (i.e., security, reliability, and dependability). Consider, for example, what it takes to design a city-scale autonomous transportation system that people can confidently use with minimal safety concerns. The committee also sees examples of gaps in today's deployed systems, such as the vulnerability to cyberattacks and poor interoperability. The following attributes and the associated design approaches and mindset are best introduced early in the CPS curriculum and infused throughout in CPS coursework and projects:

- *Security and privacy.* All information technology-based systems are subject to cyberattacks. Many CPS are especially vulnerable either because they are located in open environments or can be communicated with wirelessly. Ensuring that those designing such systems are familiar with security and privacy risks and techniques for protecting them will be crucial.

- *Interoperability.* Especially in large-scale CPS, systems will be composed of components from different vendors, and portions may be operated by different entities. Realizing the full promise of CPS will require interoperability among heterogeneous components and systems. Achieving interoperability requires knowledge of how to define and use common architectures, standardized interfaces, and data standards.
- *Reliability and dependability.* Many CPS will be part of our daily lives, and their utility will require high reliability and dependability. New problems arise because many CPS devices have limited computational power, memory, and energy. The best systems are those designed from the start with reliability (and safety) in mind—not as something to be fixed during testing. CPS will also need to be robust to uncertainties that may be difficult to quantify in the design phase. In order to make sure these uncertainties are addressed, they must be tracked and addressed during implementation stages.
- *Power and energy management.* The compact size and autonomous operation of some CPS components make energy management a critical engineering design priority.
- *Safety.* With the proliferation of CPS into daily lives, it becomes exceedingly important to ensure that actions taken on humans and the environment are safe and that the risks associated with these actions can be assessed and managed.
- *Stability and performance.* The stability of CPS, which are dynamic and stochastic systems, involves such factors as the linearity or nonlinearity of the system, the bandwidth of the systems, sampling rate, the poles and zeroes of the system, the modeling of the noise and uncertainty affecting the system, and limitations of sensors and actuators such as noise corruption or saturation.
- *Human factors and usability.* Human factors design, human-in-the-loop control, and understanding and accounting for the behavioral responses of humans are all important for many CPS applications. For instance, critical CPS are used to support the health care and well-being of the elderly.

These considerations are often essential in ensuring a system will operate with increased confidence in the presence of uncertainty and with acceptable levels of risk. The importance of improving education in these areas is highlighted by the prevalence of cyberattacks against CPS, poor usability, and lack of interoperability.

Most CPS will have to be developed with these system characteristics in mind. As a result, these concepts will need to be woven throughout a state-of-the-art CPS curriculum at all levels. The challenge in building software and hardware systems that have these properties is not unknown to the computer science and engineering domains. Exploring these challenges and learning how to determine if systems have these properties are essential to deploying better CPS.

COMPLEMENTARY SKILLS

A 2004 National Academy of Engineering (NAE) report on the future of engineering highlights the implications for engineering education of the pace of change in science and engineering knowledge and the decreasing length of product cycles.

> The comfortable notion that a person learns all that he or she needs to know in a four-year engineering program just is not true and never was. Not even the "fundamentals" are fixed, as new technologies enter the engineer's toolkit. Engineers are going to have to accept responsibility for their own continual reeducation, and engineering schools are going to have to prepare engineers to do so by teaching them how to learn.[1]

This observation is especially apt for an emerging and rapidly changing area like CPS, and suggests that CPS courses and programs need to emphasize ongoing learning and critical thinking about technology as well as specific techniques and methods.

The NAE report also takes note of the growing scale and complexity of engineering systems, which mean that engineers are increasingly working collaboratively with experts from multiple disciplines. It describes the "soft skills" needed to work effectively in such environments:

> Essential attributes for these teams include excellence in communication (with technical and public audiences), an ability to communicate using technology, and an understanding of the complexities associated with a global market and social context. Flexibility, receptiveness to change, and mutual respect are essential as well. For example, it already is found that engineers may come together in teams based on individual areas of expertise and disperse once a challenge has been addressed, only to regroup again differently to respond to a new challenge.[2]

The need for such skills is especially acute for CPS, where the engi-

---

[1] National Academy of Engineering, 2004, *The Engineer of 2020: Visions of Engineering in the New Century*, The National Academies Press, Washington, D.C., p. 24.

[2] Ibid., pp. 34-35.

neering work is inherently interdisciplinary. There are many opportunities to teach students about effective teamwork, especially in project activities culminating in a capstone project course.

Another trend in engineering education relevant to CPS is the integration of entrepreneurship. A 2013 article by Byers et al. observed that

> . . . It is no longer enough to come out of school with a purely technical education; engineers need to be entrepreneurial in order to understand and contribute in the context of market and business pressures. For engineers who start companies soon after graduation, entrepreneurship education gives them solid experience in product design and development, prototyping, technology trends, and market analysis. These skills are just as relevant for success in established enterprises as they are in startups; students with entrepreneurial training who join established firms are better prepared to become effective team members and managers and can better support their employers as innovators.[3]

Indeed, several speakers at the workshops organized for this study observed that engineering students increasingly wish to be entrepreneurial. Given the potential economic impact of CPS, related areas, and their applications, there is likely to be growing demand for integrating entrepreneurship into CPS engineering education. Entrepreneurship would naturally fit into capstone or other project-based courses.

---

[3] T. Byers, T. Seelig, S. Sheppard, and P. Weilerstein, 2013, Entrepreneurship: Its role in engineering education, *The Bridge* 43(2):35-40.

3

Paths to CPS Knowledge

Chapter 1 posits that almost all engineering fields will be impacted by the wide use of cyber-physical systems (CPS) and that the workforce will include domain experts who are knowledgeable of CPS principles, including a new type of engineer—a CPS engineer—who is an expert in the intersection of cyber and physical worlds. This suggests that multiple paths to CPS knowledge are required to meet workforce needs. It is expected that many different approaches will be undertaken depending on the situation at each university or college.

Anticipating the diverse workforce needs, the challenges associated with implementing CPS courses and programs, and a range of approaches already under way at universities, this report presents multiple alternatives. One good alternative, especially in the short term (and possibly the easiest to implement logistically) is a master's-level program. This does not obviate the need for CPS education at the B.S. level or the long-term needs for B.S.-level classes and even degrees. Given that the vast majority of engineers are hired at the B.S. level, it does not seem feasible to simply defer all CPS education to the master's level.

Ultimately, the mix of programs offered by universities will reflect the perspectives of individual institutions, their resources, and the demand universities see from students and their employers, and in turn affect the educational backgrounds of the CPS workforce. Over time, as the field itself changes and matures, education and the CPS skills that employers demand will co-evolve.

In particular, many universities may not currently have the expertise or resources to establish extensive CPS education programs. A useful alternative in these cases would be to forge more limited partnerships among several departments to implement jointly taught courses. For example, key CPS content could be introduced into mechatronics, robotics, or transportation courses. Doing so over time can help reduce the burdens associated with infusing CPS throughout engineering and building the courses one would need to implement a CPS program. For example, a theory course developed to include students from computer science and mechanical engineering, as well as traditional control theory, will produce a new class of the sort that is needed for CPS.

FINDING 3.1: The diversity of current departmental structures, faculty expertise and interests, and curricula suggest that there are multiple feasible and appropriate models for strengthening CPS engineering. The committee envisions that universities will (1) enrich current engineering programs with CPS content, (2) create CPS survey courses, (3) create new master's-level CPS degrees, and, ultimately, (4) develop new undergraduate CPS engineering degree programs.

RECOMMENDATION 3.1: The National Science Foundation should support the development of university education programs that define a path and plan for the creation of a cyber-physical systems engineering degree.

In this chapter, the committee provides examples of several paths forward. It should be emphasized that these are examples, and a wide spectrum of possible solutions from varying perspectives is anticipated. This chapter explores the following approaches to CPS knowledge:

- Exposure to CPS in K-12,
- Vocational and community college programs,
- CPS discussions in introductory engineering and computer science courses,
- One or more CPS survey courses taught at the undergraduate level,
- Domain-specific degree programs that include a CPS concentration or focus,
- A bachelor's-level CPS degree, and
- A master's-level CPS degree.

OVERVIEW OF RELEVANT EXISTING PATHS AND PROGRAMS TO CPS EXPERTISE

The committee was pleased to discover that a diverse set of CPS program models have grown organically from computer science and electrical engineering departments. Additionally, several domain areas have created programs that support the design in CPS, for example, civil engineering masters in intelligent infrastructure. Table 3.1 gives a small sampling of CPS academic offerings.

TABLE 3.1 Examples of Programs in CPS or Embedded Systems

University/Department	Sample Courses	Name of Degree
University of Pennsylvania Department of Computer and Information Science	CIS 540: Principles of Embedded Computation CIS 541: Embedded Software for Life Critical Applications	M.S. in engineering in embedded systems
Illinois Institute of Technology College of Science	CS 556: Cyber-Physical Systems: Languages and Systems CS 557: Cyber-Physical Systems: Networking and Algorithms	Master's in computer science with a specialization in cyber-physical systems
University of Colorado, Boulder Department of Electrical, Computing and Energy Engineering	ECEN 5613: Embedded System Design ECEN 5023: Mobile Computing and IoT Security	Professional master's program (30 hours) or certificate (9 hours) in embedded systems engineering
Iowa State University College of Engineering	CprE 558: Real Time Systems CprE 588: Embedded Computer Systems	Embedded systems graduate certificate
University of Illinois College of Electrical and Computer Engineering	ECE 486: Control Systems CS 431: Embedded Systems	Undergraduate concentration in cyber-physical systems
New York University School of Engineering	CS 2204: Digital Logic and State Machine Design EL 5483: Real Time Embedded Systems	Undergraduate computer science degree with a concentration in computer hardware and embedded systems
University of California, Berkeley	EECS 149.1x: Cyber Physical Systems	Open Access online course

PATHS TO CPS KNOWLEDGE 37

The few CPS degree programs that exist at present are at the graduate level, which perpetuates the belief that one must become an expert in one field before commencing study of CPS. For example, current programs require a student to complete a bachelor of science degree in either electrical and/or computer engineering before attempting to augment his or her studies with the cyber component, or complete the cyber portion first and add the physical portion afterwards.

There are a few undergraduate courses offered within existing programs that offer CPS as a concentration instead of a stand-alone degree program. Additionally, there are certification programs that complement the degree programs, as well as certification specialties.

The University of California, Santa Cruz, for example, offers an Introduction to Cyber-Physical Systems course through its College of Engineering as a part of the engineering curriculum. This class provides a basic overview of concepts and tools of CPS such as "modeling and analysis tools for continuous-time and discrete-time systems; finite state machines; stateflow; timed and hybrid automata; concurrency; invariants; linear temporal logic; verification; and numerical simulation."[1] The course provides an introduction to modeling and analysis of CPS. After the systems of interest are summarized via examples in engineering and science, several models of continuous-time systems and discrete-time systems are introduced. The main focus is on models in terms of differential equations for the modeling of physical processes. Finite state machines and stateflow are introduced and combined with the physical models. Applications of the resulting models for design and analysis of embedded systems are discussed. With this basic background, the more advanced timed automata and hybrid automata models are introduced. Then, linear temporal logic, which is the main tool taught in this class, is introduced and applied to specify the desired system behavior. Tools for analytical study and numerical verification for the satisfaction of linear temporal logic formulas are presented and discussed in numerous applications.

Another example is the University of California, Berkeley, course "Introduction to Embedded Systems," an introductory class that introduces the students to the design and analysis of computational systems that interact with physical processes. The course uses a textbook[2] written by two Berkeley faculty.

Canvassing the offerings available at most universities reveals that current courses are not sufficient to meet the need of developing engi-

---

[1] University of California, Santa Cruz, "CMPE249: Introduction To Cyber-Physical Systems," https://courses.soe.ucsc.edu/courses/cmpe249, accessed December 5, 2016.

[2] E.A. Lee and S.A. Seshia, 2015, *Introduction to Embedded Systems, A Cyber-Physical Systems Approach*, Second Edition, http://LeeSeshia.org.

neers who are adequately skilled in CPS. Few emphasize mission- or safety-critical systems, and hands-on project work tends to ignore properties like fault tolerance and robustness. Also, a focus on developing new systems over understanding tools and techniques needed to test and maintain current systems was noted. These deficiencies are due to a variety of issues, including a lack of an interdisciplinary or multidisciplinary approach, the lack application-based work, limited software engineering approaches, lack of integration, composition, and system-level concerns. Additionally, interdependencies are not accounted for in the traditional engineering coursework. In this approach, systems are broken down into components and the students design them, but they do not think about how the two are connected. In addition to these analytical skills, CPS also requires skill in synthesizing systems from understood components and integrating multiple disciplines and perspectives.

A report of a National Institute of Standards and Technology-sponsored workshop on future opportunities for CPS encourages significant enhancements to the engineering curricula in CPS degree programs, emphasizing systems sciences, engineering with an enhanced focus on multidisciplinary research.[3] Establishing multi-department CPS degrees and resources will help to build and sustain the future CPS workforce, with the goal of establishing a more formal teaching and training approach to CPS.

RECOMMENDATION 3.2: The National Science Foundation, professional societies, and university administrations should support and consider allocating resources for the development of new cyber-physical systems (CPS)-focused courses within existing engineering programs, new CPS-specific classes for CPS engineering majors and minors, and an overall curricula for an undergraduate CPS engineering degree program.

K-12 EDUCATION PROGRAMS

Strong foundations in science, technology, engineering, and mathematics (STEM) topics, coupled with exposure to CPS concepts and applications, can (1) introduce students to possible careers in CPS, (2) provide students with the foundations they will need to succeed in CPS or other STEM undergraduate programs, and (3) make it easier to fit a full CPS

---

[3] National Institute of Standards and Technology, 2013, *Strategic R&D Opportunities for 21st Century Cyber-Physical Systems: Connecting Computer and Information Systems with the Physical World*, Gaithersburg, Md., January, http://www.nist.gov/el/upload/12-Cyber-Physical-Systems020113_final.pdf.

curriculum into a 4-year course of study by giving students a head start. Both core STEM courses, such as calculus and physics, and courses on topics such as programming and robotics can all be extended with CPS content. Moreover, applications such as robotics provide timely and very attractive opportunities to motivate STEM education generally and introduce CPS content specifically. For example, the UC Davis Center for Integrated Computing and STEM Education (C-STEM) has developed a capstone course, "Principles and Design of Cyber-Physical Systems,"[4] based on use of a robotics kit, that is intended to spark interest in computing and CPS specifically. An introductory course on CPS could also be offered as a capstone of a high school career technical education course of study.

Without a robust STEM education in K-12, would-be CPS students are at a considerable disadvantage. Furthermore, given the challenges in incorporating the extensive knowledge required for CPS into a 4-year undergraduate degree, there are considerable advantages to introducing foundational material at the K-12 level. Calculus and physics are already standardized and emphasized, especially for students interested in STEM careers. By contrast, programming, robotics, and other CPS-related topics are not as well defined or institutionalized. Several efforts, most recently and broadly the "CS for All" initiative, are aimed at introducing computer science and computational thinking into K-12 education across the country and may provide opportunities to introduce CPS concepts and foundations.

VOCATIONAL AND COMMUNITY COLLEGES

Community colleges fulfill multiple roles in providing educational opportunities for students. For some, it is a pathway to a 4-year institution and a bachelor's degree. As such, students participating in engineering programs at these institutions should be made aware of CPS and the appropriate courses that will better prepare them to undertake this field of study in a 4-year program. Furthermore, these programs must be sufficiently rigorous to ensure success once entering a bachelor's program.

For others, community colleges offer vocational training for construction, auto repair, and other similar jobs. An increasing number of vocations will require an understanding of CPS fundamentals for installation and maintenance of the advanced systems that rely on CPS. These jobs, which depend on vocational education, include auto repair, HVAC installation and maintenance, and medical care. Vocational and community college education will need to evolve to develop new skills and incorpo-

---

[4] UC Davis Center for Integrated Computing and STEM Education, "C-STEM Math-ICT Pathway," http://c-stem.ucdavis.edu/curriculum/ict-pathway/, accessed November 1, 2016.

rate new knowledge to support these changing professions—as well as new fields such as design, installation, and maintenance of solar energy systems, wind turbine systems, and broadband communications systems. An example is the Washtenaw Community College,[5] which started an Advanced Transportation Center that is working to develop curricula, create opportunities for vocational training, and strengthen the community college and university interactions around connected cars and other advanced transportation systems.

People also use community colleges for the refreshment of knowledge and for retraining in technologies that have continued to evolve. Community colleges could therefore provide mid-career professionals who have already completed a degree in a related discipline (e.g., computer science, electrical engineering, or mechanical engineering) with a means to bolster their skills and capabilities in CPS knowledge. A set of the education modules could be fashioned into continuing education courses. In the event that a licensing regime for engineers is in place for these related engineering domains, it is likely that the courses so fashioned could be used to satisfy state requirements for continuing education.

UNDERGRADUATE COURSES, CONCENTRATIONS, AND PROGRAMS

This section considers various ways to incorporate CPS into undergraduate education. It starts by discussing ways to add CPS content to introductory courses for engineering and computer science undergraduates and approaches for creating survey courses that provide a more in-depth introduction to CPS. It then turns to ways to add a CPS specialization to existing engineering programs and options for creating an undergraduate program in CPS. Finally, it discusses the need for flexibility in course work, the importance of hands-on work for learning about CPS, and the need to create new courses to teach CPS.

Current engineering curricula already have extensive content with limited room for new classes, so the proposed curricula replaces existing courses with new ones designed for CPS. In the case of new concentrations in CPS, the suggested courses would replace those offered as part of existing concentrations. For example, instead of taking classes for a concentration in control, software engineering, or networking, a student would take new classes designed for a CPS concentration. In the case of a CPS degree, the example curricula include new classes that would substitute for those in the curricula from which they are derived.

---

[5] Washtenaw Community College, "Advanced Transportation Center," http://sites.wccnet.edu/atc/, accessed November 1, 2016.

Introductory Engineering and Computer Science Courses

As noted in Chapter 1, an increasing number of what was once simply physical or simply cyber systems now integrate components of each. For example, mechanical and aerospace engineers will inevitably need to incorporate their physical designs with system controls and automation. As a result, engineers will need a basic understanding of integrating the physical and cyber technologies and the complexities of building and maintaining CPS.

Most, if not all, engineering programs provide freshman engineering students with an opportunity to take introductory engineering courses. The majority of these are domain specific—each engineering department or school develops and teaches the course. The courses provide students with an overview of the field while also teaching basic engineering skills and problem solving. Given the wide deployment of CPS and the impact it has on the more traditional disciplines, the committee suggests that these courses should include discussion of the complexities of CPS and introduce some of the key CPS concepts.

The committee recognizes that these courses cover a wide set of material already; however, CPS can be woven through some of this material. For example, many of these courses include a hands-on project or a semester-long project. CPS concepts could be incorporated into these assignments by providing real-world tasks. Aerospace engineering students could work on drone control; civil engineering students could examine implications of smart cities; and mechanical engineers could explore robotics. Introducing students to the challenges of integration establishes that one does not develop systems in a vacuum and instead must consider outside impacts, including human factors, real-world constraints, and the limits of software and physics.

> **RECOMMENDATION 3.3:** Universities should consider adding cyber-physical systems content to freshman-level introductory courses for students in all areas of engineering and computer science.

New Survey Courses in CPS

Given the wide breadth of knowledge required for CPS, the structure of survey courses could take several approaches. One approach would be a class based on modules chosen from the multidisciplinary areas of CPS. Such a course could include modules on sensor networks, embedded computing, signal processing, control theory, and real-time systems. A two-course sequence might add multiple modules from security and privacy, model-based design, formal methods, hybrid systems, and data science and machine learning. In the module approach, it is emphasized that each module should not be completely independent of others, and class principles and concepts must stress the interactions across the various modules. Another approach might stress the safety critical aspects of CPS and include topics such as fault tolerance, model-based design, concurrency and distributed algorithms, models of computation, formal methods of specification and verification, real-time systems, and hybrid systems (which brings in control theory). A third approach might focus on modeling, design, and analysis—all from a multidisciplinary approach—with an explicit focus on the interdependencies between the cyber and the physical worlds. Topics might include continuous and discrete dynamics, hybrid systems, concurrent models of computation, embedded systems, multi-tasking and real-time scheduling, temporal logic, model checking, and quantitative analysis—all emphasizing integration with physical systems.

Regardless of the approach, survey courses should stress the complexities of integrating physical with cyber aspects of systems and at least touch on the foundations and system characteristics outlined in Chapter 2. Box 3.1 provides some examples of high-level undergraduate survey courses; any such listing of courses and programs represents only a sampling of an always-evolving set of courses and programs being developed and offered in the United States and worldwide. Although the topics are listed in Box 3.1, it is important to note that all of the classes include hands-on projects or laboratory work that not only emphasize course topics but also the integration of the cyber and physical worlds.

Traditional Engineering Programs with CPS Specialization

Traditional undergraduate engineering programs (e.g. aerospace, civil, mechanical, and chemical engineering, to name a few) will also benefit from the incorporation of CPS principles into their course offerings. Some fields, such as aerospace and mechanical engineering, have incorporated CPS principles for some time, but primarily from a physical world point of view. Hence, the challenge will be to increase knowledge of cyber elements and their interactions with physical elements and (1) ensure that the necessary changes to include CPS principles in the curricula meet requirements set by the Accreditation Board for Engineering and Technology (ABET) and (2) adequately prepare students to pass the National Council of Examiners for Engineering and Surveying Fundamentals of Engineering (FE) exam.

The degree to which CPS principles are currently incorporated into domain-specific curricula varies considerably depending on the discipline. Undergraduate civil and mechanical engineering curricula require students to take similar math, natural science, and basic engineering and

BOX 3.1
Examples of Survey Courses

CIS 541/441: Embedded Software for Life-Critical Applications
Insup Lee, University of Pennsylvania

This survey course is taught within the computer and information sciences department and has an emphasis on real-time issues. Current prerequisites are programming in C or Java and introduction to computer architecture or operating systems. The course also includes a series of projects that implement safety-critical embedded systems, such as a pacemaker or infusion pump.

Topics

Introduction to Cyber Physical Systems
- CPS applications
- Characteristics and challenges

Requirements, Modeling, and Analysis
- Model-based development
- Requirements capture and modeling
- State machines, timed automata
- Properties and model checking
- User mental models
- Architecture description languages
- Code generation and synthesis

Implementation Paradigms and Techniques
- Real-time operating systems
- Programming paradigms and languages
- Compositional and feedback-based real-time scheduling
- Feedback control in computer systems
- Virtual machines, hypervisors, separation kernels
- Components, plug-and-play of embedded systems
- Mixed criticality systems
- Distributed real-time systems concepts: Ordering, global time, clock synchronization
- Security and privacy

Validation, Verification, and Certification
- Testing coverage and generation
- Model-based testing
- Closed-loop testing
- Run-time monitoring and verification techniques
- Human-computer interactions
- Modular and evidence-based certification
- Hazard analysis, assurance cases

continued

BOX 3.1 Continued

Lectures

- Introduction to cyber-physical systems
- Introduction to real-time embedded systems
- Real-time operating systems, virtual machines, hypervisor
- Real-time scheduling: EDF, RM, servers, priority inversion
- Multiprocessor real-time scheduling
- Real-time programming languages and paradigms
- Distributed real-time systems: Global ordering, global time, clock synchronization
- Feedback in computer systems
- Medical cyber-physical systems
- Pacemaker challenge problem
- Assurance cases
- Medical device quality issues—FDA perspective
- Formal modeling and model checking
- Extended finite state machines, timed automata
- UPPAAL toolset: Timed automata and timed CTL, model checking
- Code generation/synthesis from state machines
- Testing, testing coverage, test generation
- Real-time testing, model-based testing, closed-loop testing
- Runtime verification
- Architecture description language, AADL
- Human-computer interaction: User interface
- User mental models
- Project presentations: Pacemaker modeling and implementation, assurance case, and demo

EECS 149/249A: Introduction to Embedded Systems
Edward A. Lee and Sanjit A. Sehsia, University of California, Berkeley

This survey course is taught within the electrical engineering and computer science school. Prerequisites include Designing Information Devices and Systems or Signals and Systems, Computer Architecture, and Discrete Mathematics. This course includes a series of hands-on laboratory work that culminates into a team project, which must relate directly to distinct topics covered in the lectures. (See https://chess.eecs.berkeley.edu/eecs149/index.html.)

Topics

Models of Computations
- Finite state machines
- Thread
- Ordinary differential equations
- Hybrid systems

- Discrete events
- Data flow

Basic Analysis, Control, and Systems Simulation
- Bisimulations
- Reachability analysis
- Controller synthesis
- Approximating continuous-time systems

Interfacing with the Physical World
- Sensor/actuator modeling and calibration
- Concurrency in dealing with multiple real-time streams
- Handling numerical imprecision in software

Mapping to Embedded Platforms
- Real-time operating systems
- Execution time analysis
- Scheduling
- Concurrency

Distributed Embedded Systems
- Protocol design
- Predictable networking
- Security

Lectures

- Cyber-physical systems overview
- Sensors and actuators
- Model-based design and continuous dynamics
- Memory architectures
- Input and output
- Modeling modal behavior and discrete dynamics
- Extended and time automata
- Composition of state machines
- Hierarchical state machines
- Specifications and temporal logic
- Comparing state machines
- Reachability analysis
- Using temporal logic in CPS autograders
- Multitasking
- Operating systems, microkernels, and scheduling
- Scheduling anomalies
- Execution time analysis
- Synchronous, reactive, and dataflow models
- Security for embedded systems
- Network-embedded systems

> **BOX 3.2**
> **Model for 4-year Undergraduate Degree in Mechanical Engineering with CPS Emphasis**
>
> **Math and Natural Sciences (9 courses)**
> - Calculus I
> - Calculus II
> - Vector Calculus
> - Differential Equations
> - Linear Algebra
> - Probability and Statistics
> - Physics I (Mechanics and Dynamics)
> - Physics II (Electricity and Magnetism)
> - General Chemistry
>
> **Traditional Mechanical Engineering Courses (13 courses)**
> - Introduction to Engineering Graphics and Design
> - Mechanics I: Statics
> - Mechanics II: Dynamics
> - Solid Mechanics
> - Fluid Mechanics
> - Thermodynamics
> - System Dynamics
> - Engineering Material Science
> - Experimental Techniques Laboratory
> - ME systems Laboratory
> - Heat Transfer
> - Design, Materials and Manufacturing
> - Engineering Economy

science courses during the first 2 years. The third year primarily focuses on introducing students to the concentration areas in their respective disciplines. As an example, within civil engineering these concentration areas include structural, geotechnical, transportation, environmental, hydrology/hydraulics, and construction engineering. Examples of mechanical engineering concentration areas include robotics and controls, thermal-fluid systems, manufacturing, and solid mechanics. In the fourth year, most students develop a specialization by focusing on one of these concentration areas through their technical electives. A capstone design course is also often part of the fourth-year curriculum.

Two example curricula are presented in Boxes 3.2 and 3.3—one for mechanical engineering and the second from civil engineering. These two

CPS-Related Courses in Current ME Curricula (5 courses)
- Introduction to Computing
- Circuits and Electronics
- Computational Methods in Engineering
- Instrumentation and Electronics Laboratory
- Capstone Design (with CPS-focused project)

Technical Electives that Could Focus on CPS (5 courses)
Proposed new CPS-centric electives:
- Principles of CPS
- Network-embedded systems programming
- Signals and Systems
- Control of Dynamic Systems
- Model-Based Systems Engineering

Examples of CPS-related electives in current ME curricula:
- Modeling and Control of Motion Control
- Microprocessor Control of Manufacturing Systems
- Robotics
- Bio-Inspired Design
- Design Across Disciplines
- Biomedical Instrumentation
- Mechatronics
- Sensor Networks

Social Science, Economics, Humanities (8 courses)

examples, based on existing curricula from several universities, show that the mechanical engineering curriculum has, to some degree, more existing CPS-focused core classes and technical electives than the civil engineering curriculum. However, these existing courses may require redesign in an effort to better introduce undergraduates to the cyber aspects of CPS and their interactions with the physical, as defined in Chapter 2.

New CPS-centric courses have been proposed in both curricula. Such courses are meant as examples only, and many more domain-specific courses with a CPS emphasis can be defined. Given the flexibility in today's ABET accreditation process, and because it is anticipated that these courses will primarily be part of the technical elective alternatives, problems meeting ABET accreditation requirements or adequately pre-

> **BOX 3.3**
> **Model for 4-Year, Undergraduate Degree in Civil Engineering with CPS Emphasis**
>
> **Math and Natural Sciences (10 courses)**
> - Calculus I
> - Calculus II
> - Vector Calculus
> - Differential Equations
> - Linear Algebra
> - Probability and Statistics
> - Physics I (Mechanics and Dynamics)
> - Physics II (Electricity and Magnetism)
> - General Chemistry
> - Science Elective (Biology or Earth Science)
>
> **Traditional Civil Engineering Courses (13 courses)**
> - Introduction to Engineering Graphics
> - Mechanics I: Statics
> - Mechanics II: Dynamics
> - Solid Mechanics
> - Fluid Mechanics
> - Thermodynamics
> - Environmental Engineering
> - Civil Engineering Materials
> - Required electives (4 classes from Structural Engineering, Construction Management, Environmental Engineering Systems, Hydraulic Engineering, Geotechnical Engineering, Transportation Engineering)
> - Engineering Economy

paring a student to pass the FE exam should be minimal. In fact, some of the "new" course topics (e.g., signals and systems, sensor networks, and structural health monitoring) already exist as electives in a few undergraduate engineering curricula. This flexibility will also allow accommodation of changes in the CPS curriculum as the field evolves.

Undergraduate Bachelor Programs in Cyber-Physical Systems

The committee provides an example of what a bachelor's degree in CPS might look like in Boxes 3.4, 3.5, and 3.6. Designing a CPS degree is

CPS-Related Courses in Current CE Curricula (3 courses)
- Computing for Engineers
- Civil Engineering Systems (needs to be developed with CPS focus)
- Capstone Design (with CPS-focused project)

Technical Electives (6 courses)

Current CE curricula have few undergraduate elective courses that focus on CPS concepts. If redesigned, some current elective courses could incorporate CPS principles, examples include the following:
- Geographic Information Systems
- Transportation Planning and Design
- Infrastructure Rehabilitation
- Environmental Geotechnology
- Subsurface Characterization
- Environmental Systems Design
- Building Information Modeling
- Conceptual Structural Design
- Computational and Graphical Tools for Structural Engineering
- Structural System Testing and Model Correlation

Proposed new CPS-centric electives:[1]
- Principles of CPS: Sustainable Infrastructure
- Principles of CPS: Urban Planning
- Signals and Systems
- Sensor Networks for Civil Engineering Systems
- Model-Based Systems Engineering
- Structural Health Monitoring

Social Science, Economics, Humanities (8 courses)

---

[1] These courses must be designed to incorporate the foundations defined in Chapter 2 of this report.

---

quite complex—even without considering resource constraints—owing to many confounding factors. Although such a curriculum would be based on the foundations and system characteristics outlined in Chapter 2, it is extremely difficult to produce a single ideal curriculum for the following chief reasons:

- It would require too many existing courses to cover CPS in sufficient depth. Hence, without careful program design, either the physical or the cyber aspects will end up with insufficient emphasis.
- One's own specialty affects one's view of an ideal curriculum. For

> **BOX 3.4**
> **One Model for 4-Year, 40-Course Undergraduate Degree in CPS**
>
> **Math and Natural Science (10 courses)**
> - Calculus I and II
> - Differential Equations
> - Linear Algebra
> - Probability and Statistics
> - Logic
> - Physics I (Mechanics and Dynamics)
> - Physics II (Electrical Circuits)
> - Chemistry or Biology
> - Discrete Math
>
> **CPS Core (12 courses)**
> - Introduction to CPS (Freshman Laboratory Course)
> - Computer Programming
> - Data Structures and Algorithms
> - Programming Physical Systems
> - Software Engineering
> - Model-Based System Design
> - Heterogeneous Models of Computation
> - Formal Methods and Synthesis
> - Resource-Aware Real-Time Computing
> - Control Systems
> - Optimization
> - Digital Signal Processing

example, to a control theory expert, a single course on control would not cover the topic to a depth they feel is necessary. A basic control course might be desired in addition to an embedded systems control course.

The committee stresses that the examples provided were developed with an understanding of these complexities and only serve as examples—not as the canonical curriculum. Caveats and important notes are provided in the next section.

Box 3.4 presents one possible example of an undergraduate CPS degree program curriculum. The example produced assumes a limit of 40 undergraduate courses so that the degree can be granted in 4 years. To support the physical foundations of CPS, a set of mathematics and natural science courses are necessary. Ten such classes are presented in Box 3.4. Flexibility should also exist to replace classes with electives if students place out of any earlier coursework. Box 3.4 also presents an example of 12 courses that could serve as the core of this new major. A particular uni-

> **Senior Capstone Design, 2 semesters (counts as 2 courses)**
> Senior capstone would include the following:
> • Industry participation
> • Interdisciplinary teams that pull from other domains, including business and management programs
>
> **CPS Electives (2 courses)**
> Possible topics: Inference under uncertainty, security, privacy, wireless sensor networks, computer architecture, operating systems, databases, data science, cloud computing, communication networks, network science, network control, resilient systems, information theory, machine learning, artificial intelligence, optimization, robotics, stochastic systems, adaptive systems
>
> **Societal Impact Electives (3 courses)**
> • Contextualize domain independent foundations to specific domains
> • Show students the sense of empowerment their CPS skill set provides
> • Ethics
> • Possible topics: Modern avionics, automotive systems, robotics, smart buildings, intelligent transportation, smart grid, medical devices, air traffic control, unmanned aerial vehicles
>
> **Social Science and Humanities (8 courses)**
> **Free Electives (3 courses)**

versity may choose to structure this material differently, but the content found in these courses is important.

Depending on the college or university, computer science and engineering may be located within the natural sciences, in engineering schools, or in schools of computing. CPS programs have already grown organically within both computer science and electrical engineering programs. The resulting CPS curricula will tend to look somewhat different depending on whether the program comes from a computer science perspective (see, for example, Box 3.5)[6] or from an electric and computer engineering perspective (see, for example, Box 3.6). Either of these curricula would provide tightly coupled physical and cyber instruction, but with different

---

[6] A CPS program based on a computer science program might not formally be housed in an engineering school if the computer science department was located in another college. However, significant interactions with engineering departments would be needed to provide a full degree that covers the physical side of CPS.

> **BOX 3.5**
> **Model For 4-Year, 40-Course Undergraduate Degree in CPS, Electrical Engineering Program**
>
> **Math and Natural Science[1,2] (11 courses)**
> - Calculus I and II
> - Differential Equations
> - Linear Algebra
> - Probability and Statistics
> - Logic
> - Physics I (Mechanics and Dynamics)
> - Physics II (Electricity and Magnetism)
> - Chemistry or Biology
> - Math Elective (Analysis, Algebra, Graph Theory)
> - Natural Sciences Elective (Statistical Physics, Biochemistry, Systems Biology)
>
> **Introduction to CPS (1 course)**
> - Freshman laboratory course emphasizing hands-on, multidisciplinary teamwork with a CPS system
>
> **Computing Foundations (5 courses)**
> - Programming Physical Systems
> - Heterogeneous Models of Computation
> - (Distributed) Algorithms
> - Formal Methods and Synthesis
> - Resource-Aware Real-Time Computing
>
> **CPS Core (7 courses)**
> - Digital Signal Processing
> - Networks

emphasis. Most universities allow for the cross-listing of courses that are applicable to electrical and computer engineering and computer science degrees, which tends to blur such distinctions and provides students with the flexibility to acquire the desired balance of perspectives as they study CPS.

Caveats and Notes on Curriculum

Flexibility in Course Work

In today's engineering schools, the need for flexibility in curricula is stressed for students. More and more universities are increasing the

- Stochastic Systems (Estimation, Detection, Inference, Adaptation)
- Model-Based System Design
- Junior Platforms Laboratory (Internet of Things Laboratory, Robotics, Sensor Network, Medical Devices)
  - Control Systems
  - Optimization

CPS Electives (choice of 3 courses)
Possible topics: Security, privacy, data science, cloud computing, networks, network control, resilient systems, information theory, machine learning, artificial intelligence, optimization, adaptive systems

Senior Capstone Design (2 semesters; counts as 2 courses)
Senior capstone would include the following:
- Industry participation
- Interdisciplinary teams that pull from other domains, including business and management programs

Societal Impact Electives (2 courses)
- Contextualize domain independent foundations to specific domains
- Show students the sense of empowerment their CPS skill set provides
- Possible topics: Modern avionics, automotive systems, robotics, smart buildings, intelligent transportation, smart grid, medical devices, air traffic control, unmanned aerial vehicles

Social Science and Humanities (7 courses)
Free Electives (2 courses)

---

[1] Broader exposure across continuous and discrete mathematics.
[2] Compressed calculus has implications for K-12.

opportunities for electives and lowering the number of prescriptive courses. Increased flexibility in engineering curriculum provides more opportunities for students to explore CPS through survey courses, engineering electives, and minors or certificates, while avoiding the accreditation issue discussed in earlier sections.

Accordingly, the committee's example curricula provide for flexibility. For example, the curriculum example depicts two CPS technical electives, three social impact electives, eight humanities, and three unrestricted electives. Flexibility also exists in how the Introduction to CPS and capstone projects are taught.

> **BOX 3.6**
> **Model For 4-Year, 40-Course Undergraduate Degree in CPS, Computer Science Program**
>
> **Math and Natural Science (11 courses)**
> - Calculus I
> - Calculus II
> - Differential Equations
> - Linear Algebra
> - Probabilities and Statistics
> - Logic
> - Discrete Math (Mathematical Foundations of CS)
> - Physics I (Mechanics and Dynamics)
> - Physics II (Electricity and Magnetism)
> - Biology or Chemistry
> - Laboratory course for physics
>
> **Introduction to CPS (1 course)**
> - Freshman laboratory course emphasizing hands-on, multidisciplinary teamwork with a CPS system
>
> **CPS Engineering Foundations (6 courses)**
> Select six from the following list:
> - Programming Physical Systems/Embedded Control Systems (after 2 programming classes)—deal with uncertainties, risk management, reliability, dependability and security
> - Networked embedded systems—including wireless network, sensor networks, real-time, and control inputs, distributed systems, and communication networks
> - Model-Based Development—modeling, logic, formal methods and synthesis, but all geared toward CPS
> - Linear, Feedback, and Control Systems
> - Digital Signal Processing
> - Stochastic Systems (Estimation, Detection, Inference, Adaptation)

Value of Laboratory and Hands-On Work

Project-based learning is becoming increasingly present in university engineering courses. CPS is particularly suited for hands-on learning activities and laboratory work, and project-based learning seems especially well suited to conveying the complexities of integrating cyber and physical issues. Reliance on theoretical training and waiting for a capstone design project at the end of an undergraduate education may fail to tie all of the concepts together adequately, so the on-going, practical application of theoretical learning to real problems is key. It is common practice

- Human-in-the-loop for CPS
- Optimization
- Circuits

CS/CPS (9 courses)
- Computer Programming, Languages, and Techniques (I and II)
- Data Structures and Algorithms
- Computer Architecture
- (Real-Time) Operating Systems
- Algorithms and Complexity
- Select three from the following list:
  — Databases (CS)
  — Networks and Security
  — Computer Networks
  — Computer Security
  — Software Engineering (CS)
  — Robotics
  — Artificial Intelligence (CS)
  — Machine Learning (CS)
  — Safety, Security, Privacy for High-Assurance CPS Applications

Senior Capstone Design (2 semesters; counts as 2 courses)
Senior capstone would include:
- Industry participation
- Interdisciplinary teams that pull from other domains, including business and management programs

Societal Impact Electives (2 courses)
- Technology and Society
- Ethics in Engineering and Science

Social Science and Humanities (7 courses)
Free Electives (2 courses)

for course syllabuses to now include classical homework, exams, and projects. Class projects aim at addressing a specific realistic problems by bringing together multiple concepts introduced in a course. In pioneering examples of project-based courses, instructors get engaged with students, mainly in the laboratory, promoting the creativity, teamwork, and effective accomplishment of final products. The students select real problems and work in teams toward building complete prototypical solutions for such problems. Students build hardware, compose new hardware from existing of hardware components, and learn to integrate the hardware with effective software to generate solutions to real problems.

In addition to class projects, students also typically complete capstone projects, wrapping up their studies into large projects requiring concept integration and teamwork among students with expertise in multiple areas. There are also examples where projects are linked across multiple courses.

> **RECOMMENDATION 3.4:** Engineering schools, by-and-large, have already redesigned their curricula to emphasize project-based learning. Because this is especially important for cyber-physical systems (CPS) education, these project-based courses should be extended to support CPS principles and foundations.

CPS-oriented project classes are particularly challenging to teach today because of the extremely rapidly changing landscape of available hardware and software. The traditional approach of defining a project mission that gets reused year after year does not work in this scenario. Teaching such project courses requires budgets for purchasing new hardware and software with regularity and requires considerable technical support and expertise to keep up with the possibilities. Such courses may only be only sustainable with significant institutional support in the form of course managers and laboratory technicians.

Need for New Courses

Simply collecting current courses into a new CPS program is not likely to be sufficient. Students will not truly be exposed to nor understand the intricacy of the interactions of the physical and cyber issues if this approach is taken. To give a simple illustration, most standard computer science courses do not cover real-time programming even though this topic is essential for building CPS, which interact with the physical world.

As another example, standard courses on control typically ignore the computational model in which the controller will be implemented. Those courses that do cover computational implementations of control systems, typically called digital control systems, generally have unrealistic models of computation. In other words, they assume either infinite computational resources or antiquated computational models. Moreover, typical introductory courses in control systems do not teach students about how to define the formal requirements needed to include control in the design flows used in modern CPS applications.

> **FINDING 3.2:** Because CPS engineering centers on the interaction of physical and cyber aspects of systems, it will often not be sufficient

to create CPS curricula by simply combining material from existing courses. New courses will need to be designed.

Because this is such an important point, it is illustrated by the following set of examples for how traditional courses could be modified to cover topics needed for CPS:

- *Control theory.* Control theory classes in electrical engineering emphasize topics such as stability, performance, optimization, and design of linear and nonlinear feedback systems. Hybrid control, an important topic for CPS, has received growing attention in these courses. Additional topics needed for CPS are the connection of control theory with networks and real-time and distributed systems, humans-in-the-loop, security, and software. Control examples can be supplemented with those from CPS that include physical, cyber, and networking elements. Knowledge of how to implement the control policies in software and address real time performance and security are needed. A redesign for a CPS course would provide enough basics and add the needed additional topics while reducing the emphasis on some traditional topics such as proofs of stability.
- *Software design and programming classes.* The examples used in traditional classes typically use nonphysical world applications that do not sufficiently consider the uncertainty, real time, and security challenges of the physical world. For CPS, it is important that students learn to program with sensors and actuators. For example, it is important to understand the properties of sensors and not have the properties hidden behind a high-level application program interface. For example, software that improperly handled transient signals from the lander touchdown sensor likely caused a Mars lander to prematurely "think" it had contacted the surface, causing it to shut down the retrorockets at quite a distance from the surface, resulting in mission failure.[7] Students must learn to program in a robust and secure fashion, including how to implement feedback controllers and use signal processing techniques of varying levels of sophistication. Applying real-time principles to system design and implementation to meet deadlines is essential. CPS software that interacts with users also needs special attention when human control can put humans or major systems at risk.
- *Probability and stochastic processes.* The basic principles of probability, uncertainty, and risk should be applied to CPS-type physical world systems, noisy sensor and signal properties, and overall risk assessment

---

[7] Jet Propulsion Laboratory, Special Review Board, 2000, *Report on the Loss of the Mars Polar Lander and Deep Space 2 Missions*, Report JPL D-18709, http://spaceflight.nasa.gov/spacenews/releases/2000/mpl/mpl_report_1.pdf, p. 26.

BOX 3.7
Model for a 1-Year M.Sci. CPS Degree

CPS Core (7 courses)
- Introduction to Cyber-Physical Systems
  —An introduction to all the core classes and how they relate to CPS
- Architectures for CPS
  —Sensors, actuators, networks, distributed computation
- Embedded and Real-Time Systems
  —Emphasis on computing reliably and timely with noisy sensor data over wired and wireless networks
- Formal Methods
  —Formal models of computation including discrete and analog computation
  —Formal specifications and verification
- Signal Processing
  —Digital signal processing on hardware and software
  —Emphasis on distributed signal processing over networks.
- Feedback Control
  —Modeling of physical and computational processes
  —Design techniques for stability, safety, liveness and other specifications
  —Implementation on hardware
- Inference under Uncertainty
  —Basics of modeling uncertainty, statistical inference, detection and estimation

Elective Classes (3 courses)
- Computer and Network Security
  —To cover attacks exploiting physical properties of computation (e.g., time, temperature, radiation)
- Hybrid Systems
  —Modeling, verification, and control of systems containing discrete and continuous components
- Networked Control Systems
  —Control over wired and wireless networks
  —Impact of delays, packet collisions, and protocols on performance
- Computer Architecture
- Systems Engineering
- Sensor Networks
- Medical Embedded Systems
- Robotics
- Machine Learning
- Modeling from Data

and management for systems composed of hardware and software operating in nondeterministic environments. Knowledge on how to use and program with concepts of probability and uncertainty for decision-making is required as well. Classes that show students how to apply key principles to CPS domains such as smart grids, jet engine control, or medical systems are of increasing importance.

GRADUATE DEGREE PROGRAMS

A handful of masters of science degrees focused on embedded systems or CPS exist. Despite the existing programs, the committee felt that providing a model curriculum would be helpful, especially given the focus on electrical engineering or computer science that many of the existing programs have. Another possibility is to add a CPS concentration to a robotics graduate program.

Box 3.7 presents a model for a M.Sc. degree that could be obtained in 1 year, although the typical student will take between 1 and 2 years to finish all the requirements while conducting some research. The classes are divided into required core classes and electives. For departments in a semester system, students would take eight classes. Students wishing to finish the M.Sc. degree in 1 year would take four classes in the fall semester and four classes in the spring semester or three classes in the fall quarter, three classes in the winter quarter, and three classes in the spring quarter. The M.Sc. degree would also require a project illustrating the challenges of designing CPS that work reliably in the real world.

4

Developing and Institutionalizing CPS Curricula

A number of things can be done to build and foster cyber-physical systems (CPS) programs that support current and future workforce needs. One is early exposure to CPS concepts and applications in K-12 and introductory college courses. Another is to build the needed teaching faculty, which is challenging because the traditional academic pipeline at many universities has few mechanisms in place that support extensive faculty commitment to an interdisciplinary field. Additionally, the resources needed to teach CPS courses, including textbooks, testbeds, and laboratory space, may be limited. This chapter discusses steps that academic institutions, industry (Box 4.1), and the National Science Foundation can take to strengthen undergraduate CPS education.

DRAWING STUDENTS TO CPS

Students are likely to be initially attracted to CPS through exposure to CPS-related technical areas such as robotics, autonomous vehicles, and the Internet of Things (IoT) or exposure to applications that address national and global problems in areas such as sustainability, environmental issues, and health. Beyond that, students may need some link to be drawn between these topics and the discipline of CPS.

As discussed in Chapter 3, a strong K-12 science, technology, engineering, and mathematics (STEM) foundation and exposure to CPS concepts and applications can help attract students and prepare them for undergraduate study in CPS. Notably, several of the K-12 STEM programs

> **BOX 4.1**
> **The Role of Industry in Evolving CPS Programs and Curricula**
>
> Although much of the work to develop cyber-physical systems (CPS) programs and curricula will take place in academia, industry can also play an important part. Potential roles for industry include the following:
>
> • Encouraging industry experts to participate as guest lecturers and adjunct and guest faculty to support the development of CPS programs;
> • Providing ongoing feedback on the design of CPS courses and curricula and on the preparation of students who work in industry as interns or new hires; and
> • Providing financial or in-kind support for developing curricular materials, programs, and testbeds that reflect the current state of art.

introduce students to CPS concepts, and many are based on robotics.[1] By using concrete CPS examples, these programs are an effective way to introduce the concepts of CPS and highlight their correlations with elements of their STEM education.

At the undergraduate level, the concepts of CPS can be reinforced by again making the link between CPS and related technology areas. As recommended in Chapter 1, this introduction to CPS can be part of freshman "introduction to engineering" programs. Faculty need not shy away from topics that pique student interest even as they stress the CPS foundations that underpin such areas.

Students, particularly those at universities, are acutely aware of job opportunities and salaries associated with various engineering disciplines. Therefore, promoting job needs and compensation for CPS graduates to high-school seniors and undergraduate and graduate students will also promote the field. Invited lecturers and from industry can help make introductory (and other CPS) courses current and compelling and also expose students to opportunities in industry.

---

[1] Examples include such as the FIRST Lego League (http://www.firstlegoleague.org/), which brings STEM robotics to younger children starting in the 4th grade, First Robotics (see http://www.usfirst.org/roboticsprograms/frc), the University of California, San Diego, COSMOS program (http://www.jacobsschool.ucsd.edu/cosmos/index.shtml), or RoboCup Junior (http://rcj.robocup.org/), accessed November 1, 2016.

FINDING 4.1: Although there are many STEM courses and programs at the high school and undergraduate level that introduce the students to some CPS elements such programs often do not provide a broad introduction to CPS foundations and principles and tend to be focused either on overly simplistic applications or on too discipline-centric content.

RECOMMENDATION 4.1: Those developing K-12 science, technology, engineering, and mathematics (STEM) programs and educating and training STEM teachers should consider opportunities to enrich these programs with cyber-physical systems (CPS) concepts and applications in order to lay intellectual foundations for future work and expose students to CPS career opportunities.

FINDING 4.2: Incoming college students appear to be unfamiliar with the term CPS, CPS concepts, and job opportunities in CPS. They are, however, drawn to courses and programs in more widely visible, CPS-related topics such as robotics, the IoT, health care, smart cities, and the Industrial Internet.

RECOMMENDATION 4.2: Those developing cyber-physical systems engineering courses and programs should consider leveraging the visibility of and student interest in areas such as robotics, the Internet of Things, health care, smart cities, and the Industrial Internet in descriptions of careers, courses, and programs and when selecting applications used in courses and projects.

RECRUITING, RETAINING, AND DEVELOPING THE NEEDED FACULTY

CPS exists not only across disciplines, but also at the intersection of various disciplines. Faculty teaching CPS foundational, specialized, or project-based courses will need to have an understanding of the multidisciplinary aspects of the CPS spectrum. CPS faculty will not only need depth in a particular aspect of CPS, but will also need the capability to relate their expertise to the other aspects of a complete CPS system and its respective domain-specific needs. The steps for recruiting, retaining, and developing the needed CPS faculty are briefly discussed below.

Recruiting

More new CPS-specific faculty will be produced as more research is pursued in the field. In the long term, the ideal faculty recruit will (1) have graduated with a CPS degree or specialization and (2) have a record of conducting CPS-specific research. Another source of faculty would be those with industrial experience in CPS technologies. It is furthermore expected that the calls for faculty positions will explicitly mention CPS education and research. In fact, even now there are already several universities that include CPS in their call for new faculty.

Currently and in the near-future before CPS education is well established, CPS faculty recruitment will require departments to look for faculty who will have both intense depth but also breadth. Recruiters will look for charismatic faculty with a high-level of initiative who will play an important role in drawing students to CPS education. Recruitment also requires the opening of teaching slots, which will inevitably lead to competition for these slots from more traditional research areas.

It must be acknowledged that the teaching capital for current students is already limited, and universities may be reluctant to add additional constraints by taking on CPS as a new discipline within existing programs. As a result, new hires tend to be limited to individuals who can support a university's current core curriculum. Therefore, developing a specific CPS degree program will create clear opportunities for hiring individuals with a teaching and research background focused specifically on CPS.

Retaining

The current academic system, in particular tenure and promotion decisions, builds strongly upon the depth in the faculty's own field and through publications that are often discipline limited. Because CPS faculty will have a broader profile of research, they may publish in a variety of venues, and the current promotion criteria may limit the development of CPS-centric faculty. However, there are a number of well-recognized conferences in CPS (e.g., CPS Week), as well as textbooks and a new Association of Computing Machinery journal *Transactions on Cyber-Physical Systems*. Such events and publication venues create a growing academic community around CPS. Young CPS faculty with a multidisciplinary profile can then establish themselves as CPS researchers and still meet the academic evaluation criteria. Interestingly, given the novelty of the area, young faculty could more easily become leaders in the CPS field, as they do not need to find a place in other more mature fields with a large number of well-established and well-recognized leaders.

Developing

Faculty members who have a proven record in their own field and then venture into this more interdisciplinary field once they achieve tenure do much of the existing CPS education and research. In the future, the committee envisions the development of new entry-level faculty as CPS educators. Given the already broad scope of this study, the committee did not explore the development of Ph.D. programs in CPS in any depth. For example, it did not consider the extent to which much of the training necessary for Ph.D. students might be covered by the educational content in master's-level programs. Nevertheless, over time, provided that demand for faculty and research funding opportunities are both sustained, it is reasonable to anticipate that institutions will start establishing Ph.D. programs in CPS. Moreover, if CPS follows the pattern of other engineering disciplines, Ph.D.-level engineers will fill important technical leadership roles in industry and more Ph.D.'s will take jobs in industry than will pursue academic careers, contributing further to demand for Ph.D. programs in CPS.

While the new specialized CPS faculty is emerging, the use of teaching modules may serve to alleviate some of the time and resource constraint placed on educators. The committee envisions that faculty experts in multiple CPS disciplines could then design and co-teach new courses or build course modules so that the students can be jointly taught the combined material. Such co-teaching opportunities will lead to the development of the co-teaching faculty as increasingly proficient CPS educators. Professional organizations such as the American Society of Engineering Educators can help promote the development of innovative teaching in CPS and develop conference tracks to promote the exchange of information about best practices in CPS education.

Industry experts can contribute to the development of CPS programs in such roles as guest lecturers and adjunct and visiting faculty. An opportunity for cross-discipline teaching arises where experts in one field partner with experts in other fields to teach a modular course.

Universities, industry, and government laboratories also must identify and reward effective CPS program mentors. For example, project-based courses where students solve well-defined problems involving real physical systems that need to be integrated with safe and secure programs will be of special significance. Students will be challenged to devise and develop solutions that actually work, and the CPS-focused research experience of undergraduates, as well as industry and government laboratory summer intern programs, will further promote the CPS discipline with undergraduates. Such programs will not be successful without dedicated mentors who can motivate students to explore CPS engineering and excite these students about their career possibilities if they choose to pursue a CPS education.

> **FINDING 4.3:** Because CPS is a new field that draws on multiple disciplines, not all institutions can be expected to have enough faculty with the requisite knowledge to teach all of the courses needed for a CPS degree program.

> **RECOMMENDATION 4.3:** The National Science Foundation should support the development of cyber-physical systems faculty through the use of teaching grants and fellowships.

CURRICULUM DEVELOPMENT AND RESOURCES

Chapter 3 lays out several options for education programs at the undergraduate level—from survey courses to full degree programs. Common features of all of these options is that new or redesigned courses will be needed in order to teach the complexities of CPS and that opportunities for hands-on work, which is key to re-enforcing key concepts and integration, is essential.

In order for universities to support new education programs, they will need the appropriate resources, including new textbooks and testbeds and laboratory space. A limited number of textbooks, curricular materials, and laboratory facilities exist to support CPS.

Few textbooks exist that provide a complete overview of CPS; these textbooks are essential to teaching well-designed survey courses. The committee was encouraged by the release of several textbooks during its work. Edward Lee and Sanjit Seshia compiled a new textbook, *Introduction to Embedded Systems: A Cyber-Physical Systems Approach*, when developing their survey course at University of California, Berkeley, because one simply did not exist that met their needs.[2] Rajeev Alur also released another text, *Principles of Cyber-Physical Systems*, in 2015.[3]

Traditional course textbooks for standard engineering courses, such as controls or signal processing, may not fully incorporate the effects of the physical system on cyber technology, and vice versa. Just as courses will need to be significantly redesigned, so will textbooks. Both may sometimes be accomplished by supplementing existing materials with CPS material, exercises, and laboratory projects.

Furthermore, CPS are often very complex and students need a full

---

[2] E.A. Lee and S.A. Seshia, 2015, *Introduction to Embedded Systems: A Cyber-Physical Systems Approach*, Second Edition, http://LeeSeshia.org.
[3] R. Alur, 2015, *Principles of Cyber-Physical Systems*, MIT Press, Cambridge, Mass.

understanding of how the physical environment impacts these systems. Realistic models can provide some of this knowledge, but hands-on engagement through project-based learning is integral to developing an understanding of CPS complexities, and participation in complex interdisciplinary projects will help develop needed systems-level thinking. Providing students with these opportunities depends on having the appropriate facilities.

Design laboratories where students can work on integrative CPS projects with multi-disciplinary teams are one option. Another is to provide students with access to testbeds that allow for the co-design of physical and computational components to demonstrate the benefits of integrating simulation and experimentation. It is also important for students to be exposed to testbeds because they are a key element of industrial practice as part of the development process. A classic example of industrial testbeds is hardware-in-the-loop, where one combines simulation and physical devices, where possible, to reduce cost and complexity and increase flexibility with physical components where simulation does not provide sufficient fidelity. Testbeds are expensive to create and maintain, and many universities do not have, or will not allocate, resources to create such testbeds. Partnerships among institutions and with industry can help share the costs and leverage existing resources, and ensure that testbeds reflect the current state of art and practice.

FINDING 4.4: If they are to teach new CPS courses and build CPS programs, universities will need to allocate time and resources to develop CPS course materials and to provide the necessary laboratory space and equipment (including both virtual and physical testbeds).

FINDING 4.5: Testbeds are needed to provide students with sufficiently realistic applications and problems. These can be both virtual and physical and can be remotely accessed and shared among multiple institutions and developed and operated in cooperation with industry.

RECOMMENDATION 4.4: The National Science Foundation, professional societies, and universities should support the development and evolution of cyber-physical systems textbooks, class modules (including laboratory modules), and testbeds. These parties should partner with industry in developing and maintaining realistic testbeds.

FOSTERING DEVELOPMENT OF THE CPS DISCIPLINE AND CPS EDUCATION

As discussed above, more can be done to raise awareness about career opportunities in CPS among prospective students. In industry, although there is growing awareness of the need for CPS skills, the full set of skills required to effectively engineer CPS is not universally appreciated.

Sustained support for research allows students to focus their graduate research on CPS, which in turn produces the next generation of entry-level faculty that can build and teach the discipline. Research also generates papers for conferences and journals and creates innovative ideas and startup spinoffs. All of these byproducts of research funding help to define CPS as an accepted discipline and raise awareness at all levels within the technical community. CPS will also become more visible as formal specializations and degree programs emerge and as CPS-trained engineers make significant contributions to industry.

Those within the field can assist by reaching out to industry, preparing materials, and participating in workshops and seminars to broaden understanding of what CPS is (and is not), the complicated nature of CPS, and what can be gained by hiring people more formally educated in the field of CPS. Such education can be passive (e.g., availability of material on websites) or active through workshops and seminars.

At universities, some of the push for CPS education will naturally occur from the bottom-up—that is, faculty making the effort to incorporate CPS material into the curriculum and develop CPS courses. However, as with any emerging interdisciplinary area, if these initiatives are to take root, the encouragement and support of university administrators will be essential. Many university administrations already promote teaching and research closely aligned with CPS, such as curricula emphasizing engineering applications with direct societal impact and engineering programs oriented toward interdepartmental teamwork and complex, real-world systems. University administrations can additionally support emerging or planned CPS education by providing the necessary personnel, laboratory space, and initiation grants.

Appendixes

A

Biographies of Committee Members and Staff

JOHN A. STANKOVIC, *Co-Chair*, is the BP America Professor in the Computer Science Department at the University of Virginia. Dr. Stankovic served as chair of the department for 8 years. He is a fellow of both the Institute of Electrical and Electronics Engineers (IEEE) and the Association for Computing Machinery (ACM). He has been awarded an honorary doctorate from the University of York. He won the IEEE Real-Time Systems Technical Committee's Award for Outstanding Technical Contributions and Leadership. Dr. Stankovic also won the IEEE Technical Committee on Distributed Processing's Distinguished Achievement Award (inaugural winner). He has seven best paper awards, including one for the ACM Conference on Embedded Networked Sensor Systems (SenSys) 2006. He also has two best paper runner up awards, including one for the ACM/IEEE Conference on Information Processing in Sensor Networks (IPSN) 2013. He has also been a finalist for four other best paper awards. Dr. Stankovic has an h-index of 107 and more than 41,000 citations. In 2015, he was awarded the University of Virginia Distinguished Scientist Award, and in 2010, the School of Engineering's Distinguished Faculty Award. Dr. Stankovic also received a distinguished faculty award from the University of Massachusetts. He has given more than 35 keynote talks at conferences and many distinguished lectures at major universities. Currently, he serves on the Computer Science Telecommunications Board of the National Academies of Sciences, Engineering, and Medicine. Dr. Stankovic was the editor-in-chief for the *IEEE Transactions on Distributed and Parallel Systems* and was founder and co-editor-in-chief for the

Real-Time Systems Journal. His research interests are in real-time systems, wireless sensor networks, wireless health, cyber-physical systems (CPS), and the Internet of Things. Dr. Stankovic received his Ph.D. from Brown University.

JAMES STURGES, *Co-Chair*, is an independent consultant specializing in program management and systems engineering for very large, complex aerospace and defense systems. He retired in 2009 from Lockheed Martin Corporation, where he had been director, engineering processes, and director, mission assurance. Prior to that, Mr. Sturges was vice president, engineering and total quality, at Loral Air Traffic Control/Lockheed Martin Air Traffic Management, and C3I Strategic Business Area director for Loral Tactical Defense Systems, Arizona. He is an associate fellow and past member of the Standards Executive Council and chair of the Systems Engineering Technical Committee of the American Institute of Aeronautics and Astronautics, and was twice chair of the Corporate Advisory Board for the International Council on Systems Engineering. Early in his career, Mr. Sturges was a naval aviator, instrument instructor and check pilot, and antisubmarine warfare officer for the U.S. Navy. He has a B.A. from the University of North Carolina and an M.S. and aeronautical engineer degree from the Naval Postgraduate School at Monterey.

ALEXANDRE BAYEN is the Liao-Cho Professor of Engineering at the University of California, Berkeley. He is a professor of electrical engineering and computer science and civil and environmental engineering and director of the Institute of Transportation Studies. He is also a faculty scientist in mechanical engineering at the Lawrence Berkeley National Laboratory. He was a visiting researcher at NASA Ames Research Center from 2000 to 2003. Between January 2004 and December 2004, he worked as the research director of the Autonomous Navigation Laboratory at the Laboratoire de Recherches Balistiques et Aerodynamiques (Ministere de la Defense, Vernon, France), where he holds the rank of major. Dr. Bayen has authored two books and more than 150 articles in peer-reviewed journals and conferences. He is the recipient of the Ballhaus Award from Stanford University (2004) and the CAREER award from the National Science Foundation (2009), and he is a NASA Top 10 Innovator on Water Sustainability (2010). His projects Mobile Century and Mobile Millennium received the 2008 Best of ITS Award for Best Innovative Practice at the ITS World Congress and a TRANNY Award from the California Transportation Foundation (2009). Mobile Millennium has been featured more than 200 times in the media, including TV and radio (CBS, NBC, ABC, CNET, NPR, KGO, the BBC) as well as in the popular press (*Wall Street*

Journal, Washington Post, LA Times). Dr. Bayen is the recipient of the Presidential Early Career Award for Scientists and Engineers (PECASE) from the White House (2010) and the recipient of the Okawa Research Grant Award, the Ruberti Prize from IEEE, and the Huber Prize from ASCE. He received an engineering degree in applied mathematics from the Ecole Polytechnique, France; an M.S. degree in aeronautics and astronautics from Stanford University; and a Ph.D. in aeronautics and astronautics from Stanford University.

CHARLES R. FARRAR is the Engineering Institute leader at Los Alamos National Laboratory (LANL) and a laboratory fellow. This institute is a research and education collaboration between LANL and the University of California, San Diego (UCSD) Jacobs School of Engineering with a research focus on multi-disciplinary projects that integrate advanced predictive modeling, novel sensing systems, and new approaches to information technology. He has 33 years' experience at LANL. Dr. Farrar's research interests focus on developing integrated hardware and software solutions for monitoring the health of structures. The results of this research have been documented in more than 400 publications as well as numerous keynote lectures at international conferences. Additional professional activities include an associate editor position for *Earthquake Engineering and Structural Dynamics* and the development of a short course entitled "Structural Health Monitoring: A Statistical Pattern Recognition Approach," which has been offered more than 30 times at conferences and to industry and government agencies in Asia, Australia, Europe, and the United States. Dr. Farrar is also an adjunct professor in the Structural Engineering Department at UCSD where he teaches a graduate course on structural health monitoring. In 2007, he was elected a fellow of the American Society of Mechanical Engineers. He received a Ph.D. in civil engineering from the University of New Mexico in 1988.

MARYE ANNE FOX is the former chancellor of UCSD. She has received honorary degrees from 12 institutions in the United States and abroad, and in October 2010, President Barack Obama awarded Dr. Fox the National Medal of Science, the highest honor bestowed by the U.S. government on scientists, engineers, and inventors. Previously, she was chancellor at North Carolina State University, and she spent 22 years at the University of Texas where she advanced to vice president for research and held the Waggoner Regents Chair in Chemistry. Dr. Fox is a member of the National Academy of Sciences. She earned a bachelor's degree in science from Notre Dame College, a master's degree in science from Cleveland State University, and a Ph.D. in Chemistry from Dartmouth College.

SANTIAGO GRIJALVA is an associate professor of electrical and computer engineering at the Georgia Institute of Technology. He joined the faculty in 2009. He is the director of the Advanced Computational Electricity Systems Laboratory, where he conducts research on real-time power system control, informatics, and economics, and renewable energy integration in power. In 2012, Dr. Grijalva was appointed as the Strategic Energy Institute associate director for electricity systems, responsible for coordinating large efforts on electricity research and policy at Georgia Tech. He was a post-doctoral fellow in power and energy systems at the University of Illinois from 2003 to 2004. From 1995 to 1997, he was with the Ecuadorian National Center for Energy Control as engineer and manager of the Real-Time EMS Software Department. From 2002 to 2009, he was with PowerWorld Corporation as a senior software architect and developer of innovative real-time and optimization applications used today by utilities, control centers, and universities in more than 60 countries. Dr. Grijalva is a leading researcher on ultra-reliable architectures for critical energy infrastructures. He has pioneered work on decentralized and autonomous power system control, renewable energy integration in power, and unified network models and applications. He is currently the principal investigator of various future electricity grid research projects for the Department of Energy, the Advanced Research Projects Agency-Energy, the Electric Power Research Institute, and the Power Systems Engineering Research Center, as well as other government organizations, research consortia, and industrial sponsors. Dr. Grijalva received the electrical engineer degree from Escuela Politécnica Nacional (EPN)-Ecuador in 1994, the M.S. certificate in information systems from Universidad de las Fuerzas Armadas (ESPE)-Ecuador in 1997, and M.S. and Ph.D. degrees in electrical engineering from the University of Illinois, Urbana-Champaign, in 1999 and 2002, respectively.

HIMANSHU KHURANA is the senior manager for the Integrated Security Technologies section of the Knowledge Systems Laboratory at Honeywell Automation and Control Systems. The Integrated Security Technologies section focuses on research, development, and technology transition in cybersecurity, computer vision, surveillance, and biometrics. Dr. Khurana's research interests lie in the area of distributed system security, especially as applied to large-scale distributed systems and critical infrastructures, and he has published 50 articles in this area. Prior to joining Honeywell, he was with the University of Illinois, Urbana-Champaign, and served as the co-principal investigator for the Trustworthy Cyber Infrastructure for Power Center (now the TCIPG). He has been involved with several smart grid initiatives, including the North American Synchrophasor Initiative, the National Institute of Standards and Technology Cyber Security Working Group, DNP3 Technical Committee, and in developing relevant cyber security standards. He obtained his M.S. and Ph.D. from the University of Maryland, College Park.

PANGANAMALA R. KUMAR, professor of electrical and computer engineering at Texas A&M University, obtained his B. Tech. degree in electrical engineering (electronics) from the Indian Institute of Technology (IIT) Madras in 1973, and the M.S. and D.Sc. degrees in systems science and mathematics from Washington University, St. Louis, in 1975 and 1977, respectively. From 1977-1984, Dr. Kumar was a faculty member in the Department of Mathematics at the University of Maryland, Baltimore County. From 1985-2011 he was a faculty member in the Department of Electrical and Computer Engineering and the Coordinated Science Laboratory at the University of Illinois, Urbana-Champaign. Currently, he is at Texas A&M University, where he is a university distinguished professor and holds the College of Engineering chair in computer engineering. Dr. Kumar has worked on problems in game theory, adaptive control, stochastic systems, simulated annealing, neural networks, machine learning, queueing networks, manufacturing systems, scheduling, wafer fabrication plants, and information theory. His current research is focused on stochastic systems, energy systems, wireless networks, secure networking, automated transportation, and CPS. Dr. Kumar is a member of the U.S. National Academy of Engineering (NAE) and the World Academy of Sciences. He was awarded an honorary doctorate by ETH in Zurich. He received the IEEE Field Award for Control Systems, the American Automatic Control Council (AACC) Donald P. Eckman Award, the Fred W. Ellersick Prize of the IEEE Communications Society, the Outstanding Contribution Award of the ACM Special Interest Group on Mobility of Systems, Users, Data and Computing (SIGMOBILE), the Infocom Achievement Award, and SIGMOBILE Test-of-Time Paper Award. He is a fellow of IEEE and an ACM fellow. He was a guest chair professor and leader of the Guest Chair Professor Group on Wireless Communication and Networking at Tsinghua University, Beijing, China. He is a D. J. Gandhi Distinguished Visiting Professor at IIT Bombay. He is an honorary professor at IIT Hyderabad. He was awarded the Distinguished Alumnus Award from IIT Madras, the Alumni Achievement Award from Washington University in St. Louis, and the Daniel C. Drucker Eminent Faculty Award from the College of Engineering at the University of Illinois.

INSUP LEE is the Cecilia Fitler Moore Professor of Computer and Information Science and director of PRECISE Center, which he founded in 2008, at the University of Pennsylvania. He also holds a secondary appointment in the Department of Electrical and Systems Engineering.

Dr. Lee received a B.S. degree with honors in mathematics from the University of North Carolina, Chapel Hill, in 1977, and a Ph.D. degree in computer science from the University of Wisconsin, Madison, in 1983. His research interests include CPS, real-time systems, embedded and hybrid systems, formal methods and tools, high-confidence medical device systems, run-time verification, software certification, and trust management. The theme of his research activities has been to assure and improve the correctness, safety, and timeliness of life-critical embedded systems. Dr. Lee and his student received the best paper award at the IEEE Real-Time Systems Symposium (RTSS) 2003 on compositional schedulability analysis. His papers also received the best paper award in IEEE RTSS 2012, the best student paper at the IEEE Real-Time and Embedded Technology and Applications Symposium 2012, and the co-best paper at the Eighth Annual Collaboration, Electronic Messaging, Anti-Abuse, and Spam Conference (CEAS) 2011. Recently, he has been working in medical CPS and security of CPS. He has served on many program committees and chaired several international conferences and workshops, including IEEE RTSS, IEEE RTCSA (International Conference on Embedded and Real-Time Computing Systems and Applications), IEEE ISORC (International Symposium on Real-Time Computing), CONCUR (International Conference on Concurrency Theory), ACM EMSOFT (International Conference on Embedded Software), ACM/IEEE ICCPS (International Conference on Cyber-Physical Systems), and HCMDSS/MD PnP (High Confidence Medical Devices, Software, and Systems and Medical Device Plug-and-Play Interoperability). Dr. Lee has also served on various steering and advisory committees of technical societies, including CPS Week, Embedded Systems Week, ACM Special Interest Group on Embedded Systems, IEEE Technical Committee on Real-Time Systems (TC-RTS), RV (Runtime Verification), and ATVA (Automated Technology for Verification and Analysis). He has served on the editorial boards on the several scientific journals, including *IEEE Transactions on Computers*, *Formal Methods in System Design*, and *Real-Time Systems Journal*. He is a founding co-editor-in-chief of *KIISE Journal of Computing Science and Engineering* since 2007. He was chair of IEEE Computer Society Technical Committee on Real-Time Systems (2003-2004) and an IEEE Computer Science Distinguished Visitor Speaker (2004-2006). Dr. Lee was a member of Technical Advisory Group of President's Council of Advisors on Science and Technology Networking and Information Technology (2006-2007). He received an appreciation plague from Ministry of Science, IT and Future Planning, South Korea, for speaking at the Universal Linkage for Top Research Advisor (ULTRA) Program Forum in 2013. He is an IEEE fellow and received an IEEE TC-RTS Outstanding Technical Achievement and Leadership Award in 2008.

WILLIAM MILAM is a technical expert at the Ford Research and Innovation Center, Ford Motor Company. His research addresses modeling and implementation of advanced technology automotive engines for improved fuel economy and emissions, and improvements in systems engineering processes for the design of automotive embedded systems. He is a senior member of the IEEE and a member of SAE International (formerly the Society of Automotive Engineers). Mr. Milam serves as a member of the SAE Electronic Design Automation Standards Committee and the SAE Architecture Analysis and Design Language Standards Committee and chairs the SAE Model Based Embedded Systems Engineering Task Force.

SANJOY K. MITTER received his Ph.D. degree from the Imperial College of Science and Technology in 1965. He taught at Case Western Reserve University from 1965 to 1969. He joined the Massachusetts Institute of Technology (MIT) in 1969 where he has been a professor of electrical engineering since 1973. Dr. Mitter was the director of the MIT Laboratory for Information and Decision Systems from 1981 to 1999. He has also been a professor of mathematics at the Scuola Normale, Pisa, Italy, from 1986 to 1996. He has held visiting positions at Imperial College, London; University of Groningen, Holland; INRIA, France; Tata Institute of Fundamental Research, India and ETH, Zürich, Switzerland; and several American universities. In 2012, Dr. Mitter was the Ulam Scholar at LANL and the John von Neumann Visiting Professor in Mathematics at the Technical University of Munich, Germany. He was awarded the AACC Richard E. Bellman Control Heritage Award in 2007. He was the McKay Professor at the University of California, Berkeley, in 2000 and held the Russell-Severance-Springer Chair in fall 2003. He is a fellow of IEEE and a member of the NAE. Dr. Mitter is the winner of the 2000 IEEE Control Systems award. He was elected a foreign member of Istituto Veneto di Scienze, ed Arti, in 2003. His current research interests are communication and control in a networked environment, the relationship of statistical and quantum physics to information theory and control, and autonomy and adaptiveness for integrative organization.

JOSÉ M.F. MOURA is the Philip and Marsha Dowd University Professor of Electrical and Computer Engineering at Carnegie Mellon University (CMU), and, by courtesy, a professor of biomedical engineering. He is a member of the NAE, a fellow of the U.S. National Academy of Inventors, a corresponding member of the Portugal Academy of Science, an IEEE fellow, and a fellow of the American Association for the Advancement of Science (AAAS). Dr. Moura has been a visiting professor at New York University (2013-2014), a visiting professor at MIT (2006-2007, 1999-2000, and 1984-1986), a visiting scholar at the University of Southern California (Summers of 1979-1981), and was on the faculty of Instituto Superior Técnico (IST) (Portugal). His research interests are in data science and statistical signal and image processing. Two of his patents (co-inventor Alec Kavcic) are found in more than 3 billion hard drives of over 60 percent of all computers sold since 2003 and were the subject of a $750 million settlement in 2016 between CMU and Marvell. Current research projects include data analytics for unstructured big data, distributed inference in networks, SPIRAL (an intelligent compiler), nondestructive health-monitoring systems, bioimaging, signal processing on Graphs, and image/video processing. Dr. Moura's work has been sponsored by Defense Advanced Research Projects Agency, National Institutes of Health, Office of Naval Research, Army Research Office, Air Force Office of Scientific Research, and National Science Foundation (NSF) grants and several industrial grants. Dr. Moura received the IEEE Signal Processing Society Award for outstanding technical contributions and leadership in signal processing and the IEEE Signal Processing Society Technical Achievement Award for fundamental contributions to statistical signal processing. He is vice president for technical activities and serves on the board of directors of the IEEE, served as IEEE Division IX director (2012-2013), and was the president of the IEEE Signal Processing Society (2008-2009). He was editor-in-chief of *IEEE Transactions on Signal Processing*, acting editor-in-chief for *IEEE Signal Processing Letters*, and was on the editorial board of *ACM Transactions on Sensor Networks* and *IEEE Proceedings*. He served on several IEEE boards, including the Education Activities Board (2010) and the IEEE Technical Activities Board (TAB) (2008-2009). He holds D.Sc. and M.Sc. degrees in electrical engineering from MIT and an electrical science degree from IST (Portugal).

GEORGE J. PAPPAS is the Joseph Moore Professor and Chair of the Department of Electrical and Systems Engineering at the University of Pennsylvania. He also holds a secondary appointment in the Departments of Computer and Information Sciences, and Mechanical Engineering and Applied Mechanics. He is member of the GRASP Laboratory and the PRECISE Center. Dr. Pappas has previously served as deputy dean for research in the School of Engineering and Applied Science. His research focuses on control theory and, in particular, hybrid systems; embedded systems; hierarchical and distributed control systems, with applications to unmanned aerial vehicles; distributed robotics; green buildings; and biomolecular networks. He is a fellow of IEEE and has received various awards, such as the Antonio Ruberti Young Researcher Prize, the George S. Axelby Award, and the NSF PECASE. Dr. Pappas received his Ph.D. from the University of California, Berkeley, in 1998.

PAULO TABUADA is a professor of electrical engineering and vice chair for graduate affairs at the University of California, Los Angeles (UCLA). Between January 2002 and July 2003, he was a postdoctoral researcher at the University of Pennsylvania. After spending 3 years at the University of Notre Dame as an assistant professor, he joined the Electrical Engineering Department at UCLA, where he established and directs the Cyber-Physical Systems Laboratory. Dr. Tabuada's research interests include modeling, analysis, design, control, and security of CPS. He received his "Licenciatura" degree in aerospace engineering from IST (Portugal) in 1998 and his Ph.D. degree in electrical and computer engineering in 2002 from the Institute for Systems and Robotics, a private research institute associated with IST. Dr. Tabuada's contributions to CPS have been recognized by multiple awards, including the NSF CAREER award in 2005, the AACC Donald P. Eckman Award in 2009, and the IEEE Control Systems Society George S. Axelby Outstanding Paper Award in 2011. In 2009, he co-chaired the International Conference Hybrid Systems: Computation and Control (HSCC'09), and in 2012, he was program co-chair for the 3rd International Federation of Automatic Control Workshop on Distributed Estimation and Control in Networked Systems (NecSys'12). He also served on the editorial board of *IEEE Embedded Systems Letters* and *IEEE Transactions on Automatic Control*. His latest book, *Verification and Control of Hybrid Systems: A Symbolic Approach*, was published in 2009.

MANUELA M. VELOSO is the Herbert A. Simon Professor in the Computer Science Department, School of Computer Science, at CMU and the department head of the Machine Learning Department. She holds courtesy appointments in the Robotics Institute, the Electrical and Computer Engineering Department, and Mechanical Engineering Department. Dr. Veloso researches in artificial intelligence and robotics. She founded and directs the CORAL research group for the study of multiagent systems where agents collaborate, observe, reason, act, and learn. Dr. Veloso is a fellow of IEEE, AAAS, and the Association for the Advancement of Artificial Intelligence (AAAI). She was president of AAAI and president of the RoboCup Federation. She received the 2009 ACM/SIGART Autonomous Agents Research Award for her contributions to agents in uncertain and dynamic environments, including distributed robot localization and world modeling, strategy selection in multiagent systems in the presence of adversaries, and robot learning from demonstration. Dr. Veloso and her students have contributed a variety of autonomous robots, for robot soccer, education, and service robots. More recently, she introduced symbiotic robot autonomy, in which robots are autonomous but aware of their perceptual, cognitive, and actuation limitations and can proactively ask for help from humans, other robots, and the web. For the past 3 years, following robust localization, task planning, and symbiotic autonomy, her collaborative service robots, CoBots, have navigated for more than 1,000 km in the multifloor buildings at CMU. Dr. Veloso holds a Ph.D. in computer science from CMU and B.Sc. and M.Sc. degrees in electrical and computer engineering from IST (Portugal).

Staff

JON EISENBERG is director of the Computer Science and Telecommunications Board (CSTB) of the National Academies. He has also been study director for a diverse body of work, including a series of studies exploring Internet and broadband policy and networking and communications technologies. In 1995-1997 he was a AAAS Science, Engineering, and Diplomacy fellow at the U.S. Agency for International Development, where he worked on technology transfer and information and telecommunications policy issues. Dr. Eisenberg received his Ph.D. in physics from the University of Washington and B.S. in physics with honors from the University of Massachusetts, Amherst.

VIRGINIA BACON TALATI is a program officer for the CSTB. She formerly served as a program associate with the Frontiers of Engineering program at the NAE. Prior to her work at the National Academies, she served as a senior project assistant in education technology at the National School Boards Association. Ms. Bacon Talati has a B.S. in science, technology, and culture from the Georgia Institute of Technology and an M.P.P. from George Mason University, with a focus in science and technology policy.

SHENAE BRADLEY is an admistrative assistant at the CSTB. She currently provides support for the Committee on Sustaining Growth in Computing Performance, the Committee on Wireless Technology Prospects and Policy Options, and the Computational Thinking for Everyone: A Workshop Series Planning Committee, to name a few. Prior to this, she served as an administrative assistant for the Ironworker Management Progressive Action Cooperative Trust and managed a number of Apartment Rental Communities for Edgewood Management Corporation in the Maryland/DC/ Delaware metropolitan areas.

CHRISTOPHER JONES was an associate program officer for the CSTB. He joined the National Academies in 2016 as a Mirzayan Science and Technology Policy Fellow for the Board on Science, Technology, and Economic Policy. Prior to this, he was a start-up founder working in the connected car and energy efficiency domain, a White House fellow working on material science and water issues, and a Fulbright grantee assessing heavy metal contaminant removal technologies for drinking water. Dr. Jones received his Ph.D. and M.A. degrees from Rice University and B.S. from the Florida State University, all in chemistry.

B

Briefers to the Study Committee

COMMITTEE MEETING—JANUARY 13, 2014

David Corman, National Science Foundation

WORKSHOP—APRIL 30, 2014

Alex Bayen, University of California, Berkeley
Dick Bulterman, FXPAL
David Corman, National Science Foundation
Ryan Izard, Clemson University
Dan Johnson, Honeywell
Himanshu Khurana, Honeywell International
Jean-Charles Lede, Defense Advanced Research Projects Agency
Kevin Massey, Defense Advanced Research Projects Agency
John Mills, SimuQuest
Sanjai Rayadurgam, University of Minnesota
Joe Salvo, GE Research
Alberto Sangiovanna-Vincentelli, University of California, Berkeley
Lucio Soibelman, University of Southern California
Craig Stephens, Ford Research and Advanced Engineering
Janos Sztipanovits, Vanderbilt University
Paulo Tabuada, University of California, Los Angeles
Jon Williams, John Deere

APPENDIX B

COMMITTEE MEETING—JUNE 26, 2014

Daniel Dvorak, Jet Propulsion Laboratory

WORKSHOP—OCTOBER 2-3, 2014

Tarek Abdelzaher, University of Illinois, Urbana-Champaign
Douglas Adams, Vanderbilt University
Steve Anton, Tennessee Technological University
Harry Cheng, University of California, Davis
André DeHon, University of Pennsylvania
Magnus Egerstedt, Georgia Institute of Technology
Norman Fortenberry, American Society for Engineering Education
Christopher Gill, Washington University
Scott Hareland, Medtronic
Jonathan How, Massachusetts Institute of Technology
Clas Jacobson, United Technologies Corporation
Philip Koopman, Carnegie Mellon University
Edward Lee, University of California, Berkeley
Jerry Lynch, University of Michigan
Dimitri Mavris, Georgia Institute of Technology
Shankar Sastry, University of California, Berkeley
Henning Schulzrinne, Columbia University

COMMITTEE MEETING—MARCH 12-13, 2015

Ryan Kastner, University of California, San Diego
Yoky Matsuoka, Twitter
Astro Teller, Google, Inc.
Feng Zhao, Microsoft Research Asia

C

Workshop Agendas

APRIL 30, 2014
NATIONAL ACADEMY OF SCIENCES
WASHINGTON, D.C.

The goal for this workshop is to gain an understanding of the need for cyber physical systems workers, the impact of CPS on various sectors, core skills and knowledge, and educational barriers. Questions include:

- What are CPS, and how does it relate to engineering, computer science, and other related disciplines?
- What role do CPS play in sustaining innovation and supporting U.S. competitiveness and economic growth?
- What sorts of jobs require CPS knowledge and skills? (e.g., engineering design, test and evaluation, operations)
- Where does one find this talent today? How much of the needed knowledge and skills are covered in undergraduate degree programs or graduate education? How much on-the-job training is required?
- What are the core knowledge areas, capabilities, and skills that individuals working in CPS-intensive fields need? How do they map onto traditional undergraduate degree programs and courses in engineering and computer science? What areas are covered in graduate programs and courses?
- Where are there gaps in courses, textbooks and other course materials, teaching tools, curricula, and degree programs?
- What are the barriers in the educational pipeline to developing needed CPS knowledge, skills, and capabilities?

8:30 a.m.	**Introduction and Welcome** *Jack Stankovic, University of Virginia, Co-Chair* *Jim Sturges, Lockheed Martin (retired), Co-Chair*
8:45	**The Importance of Cyber Physical Systems** *Moderator: Jack Stankovic* *Panelists: David Corman, National Science Foundation* *Janos Sztipanovits, Vanderbilt University [remotely]* *Joe Salvo, GE Research*

- What are CPS, and how does it relate to engineering, computer science, and other related disciplines?
- What are some of the key applications of CPS? How do CPS help advance economically or societally important capabilities?
- What sectors will depend most on CPS-enabled capabilities?
- What role do CPS play in sustaining innovation and supporting U.S. competitiveness and economic growth?

10:00	Break
10:15	**Current and Anticipated Workforce Needs** *Moderator: Bill Milam* *Panelists: Dick Bulterman, FXPAL* *Lucio Soibelman, University of Southern California* *Craig Stephens, Ford Research and Advanced Engineering* *Jon Williams, John Deere*

- What sorts of jobs require CPS knowledge and skills? (e.g., engineering design, test and evaluation, operations)
- Where does one find this talent today? How much of the needed knowledge and skills are covered in undergraduate degree
- programs or graduate education? How much on-the-job training is required?
- What are expectations for the future size of the CPS workforce, in total or as a share of total positions?
- How important is it to have a workforce of sufficient capacity and capability?

12:00 p.m.   Lunch

1:00   **Knowledge , Capabilities, and Skills Needed in a CPS Workforce**
Moderator: Insup Lee
Panelists: Dan Johnson, Honeywell [remotely]
*   Kevin Massey, Defense Advanced Research Projects Agency*
*   John Mills, SimuQuest*
*   Sanjai Rayadurgam, University of Minnesota*
*   Alberto Sangiovanni-Vincentelli, University of California, Berkeley*

Each sector deploying cyber-physical systems has tended to work independently of others in developing the necessary science, engineering, workplace skills, and regulatory approach—reflecting in part the historically modest "cyber content" of most systems and organic efforts to solve the problems at hand. Today, there is growing interest in seeking advances with common application in science and engineering (including scientific and engineering principles, algorithms, models, and theories); tools (including programming languages and tools for reasoning about the properties of CPS); and building blocks (innovative hardware and software components, infrastructure, and platforms).

- What knowledge and skills are common across sectors? What are sector-specific?
- What are the core knowledge areas, capabilities, and skills that individuals working in CPS-intensive fields need? How do they map onto traditional undergraduate degree programs and courses in engineering and computer science?
- What areas are covered in graduate programs and courses?
- Where are there gaps between what is taught and what employers need?
- How do employees lacking needed knowledge or skills acquire them? How do employers provide these education and training opportunities to their employers?

2:30   Break

2:45 **Challenges and Opportunities in CPS Education**
Moderator: Sanjoy Mitter
*Panelists: Alex Bayen, University of California, Berkeley
Ryan Izard, Clemson University
George Pappas, University of Pennsylvania*

To make progress in the CPS education pipeline, it will be important to understand the nature of current barriers and to develop strategies to overcome them. One challenge is the multidisciplinary character of educational foundations for CPS literacy. Looking across computer science, electrical engineering, and other engineering disciplines will be critical. Moreover, the audience for education in CPS is not found only in a traditional academic context where disciplines and knowledge are relatively settled. The challenges also include re-educating today's faculty, devising new preparation paths for university computer science and engineering students, upgrading K-12 teachers and the K-12 pipeline, as well as the existing workforce. New modalities for lab-centric, team-taught, and online education are emerging, which merit investigation as potential tools for accelerating progress toward a more CPS-capable workforce and society.

- Where are there gaps in courses, textbooks and other course materials, teaching tools, curricula, and degree programs?
- What initiatives are underway to address perceived gaps? How can we assess their impact?
- What are some of the obstacles that need to be overcome? Can courses and programs be realigned as needed? Do we have the
- faculty needed to teach CPS material?
- Does our K-12 educational system provide the necessary foundation for later CPS education and work?
- What are the barriers in the educational pipeline to developing needed CPS knowledge, skills, and capabilities?
- What are some current programs/projects that are being developed to address these challenges?

4:00 Break

4:15	**Summary and Discussion** *Moderator: Jim Sturges*
	Panelists: Chuck Farrar, Los Alamos Laboratories
	              Himanshu Khurana, Honeywell International
	              Paulo Tabuada, University of California, Los Angeles

5:30	Adjourn

OCTOBER 2-3, 2014
NATIONAL ACADEMY OF SCIENCES
WASHINGTON, D.C.

The first workshop focused on identifying CPS educational requirements. This workshop is focused on identifying solutions. Questions examined include:

- Would there be a CPS engineer? Would there be a major in CPS? If it's run out of an ECE department, what would it look like? If it was run out of a CS department, what would it look like? Should it not be run out of a single department? Should it be run out of more complicated, coordinated multidisciplinary departments?
- Should it just be the four-year electives, so it's kind of a concentration rather than a whole major?
- What happens in an aerospace department or a mechanical or civil engineering or chemical?
- What should we be doing in community colleges, if anything, or high schools or K-12?

October 2, 2014

9:00 a.m.	**Introduction and Welcome** *Jack Stankovic, University of Virginia, Co-Chair* *Jim Sturges, Lockheed Martin (retired), Co-Chair*
9:30	**Current and Anticipated Workforce Needs** *Presenter:* Scott Hareland, Medtronics
10:00	Break
10:00	**Innovative Trends in Engineering Education** *Presenter:* Norman Fortenberry, American Society for Engineering Education

11:00	**Incorporating CPS Knowledge into Existing Engineering Curricula** *Moderator: George Pappas* **—Civil Engineering** *Presenter: Douglas Adams, Chair, Civil and Environmental Engineering, Vanderbilt University* **—Aerospace** *Presenter: Jonathan How, Massachusetts Institute of Technology*
12:00 p.m.	**Lunch Breakout Sessions** 1. Envisioning an undergraduate degree program in CPS: What knowledge and course work would make up a CPS degree program? How much of this course work is new versus existing courses? What course work might be displaced by CPS-centric courses? 2. Discipline-centric CPS knowledge: How will CPS be incorporated into existing disciplines, such as civil or aerospace engineering? 3. Engineering- and CS-wide core knowledge: What core knowledge in CPS should be a part of all engineering and computer science curriculum? What course work might be displaced by CPS-centric course work?
2:00	**Teaching Courses for CPS** *Presenter: André DeHon, University of Pennsylvania* • How will courses taught for CPS differ from course taught to a more general audience (i.e. classic control course verse control course for CPS)?
2:15	**Including CPS Core Knowledge into General Engineering Education** *Presenter: Shankar Sastry, University of California, Berkeley [remotely]*
3:15	**CPS Outside/Beyond 4-year Degree Programs** *Moderator: Bill Milam* **—Introducing CPS in High School** *Presenter: Harry Cheng, University of California, Davis* **—Online Education/MOOCS** *Presenter: Magnus Egerstedt, Georgia Tech*

4:30	**Critical Knowledge: Lessons from Teaching a Course and Writing a Textbook** *Presenter: Edward Lee, University of California Berkeley [remotely]*
5:30	Reception

October 3, 2014

8:30 a.m.	**Teaching for CPS** (continued) *Moderator: Manuela Veloso* *Panelists: Trek Abdelzaher, University of Illinois at Urbana-Champaign* *Henning Schulzrinne, Columbia University*

- How will courses taught for CPS differ from course taught to a more general audience (i.e., classic control course verse control course for CPS)?

9:15	**Building Current and Future Faculty** *Moderator: Paulo Tabuada* *Panelists: Jerry Lynch, University of Michigan* *Philip Koopman, Carnegie Mellon University* *Christopher Gill, Washington University*

- How do we create the teaching and research capacity needed to support CPS education?
- What are barriers to hiring faculty for CPS?
- What other resources are needed to support CPS education?

10:15	Break
10:30	Breakout Group Report Back
11:00	**Industry Exposure, Research Projects, and** *Moderator: Chuck Farrar* **Project-Based Learning** *Panelists: Dimitri Mavris, Georgia Institute of Technology* *Clas Jacobson, United Technologies Corporation* *Steve Anton, Tennessee Technological University*

- How do we measure and document the value of extracurricular activities?
- How to best incorporate project-based learning curriculum into degree programs?
- What is the role of industry-academic partnerships, co-ops, and internships?

12:30 p.m. **Wrap Up Discussion**
Jack Stankovic, University of Virginia, Co-Chair
Jim Sturges, Lockheed Martin (retired), Co-Chair